MY NEXT BREATH

MY NEXT BREATH

A MEMOIR

JEREMY RENNER

FLATIRON
BOOKS
NEW YORK

www.flatironbooks.com

Designed by Steven Seighman

Library of Congress Control Number: 2025930764

ISBN 978-1-250-38353-2 (hardcover)
ISBN 978-1-250-38354-9 (ebook)

Our books may be purchased in bulk for promotional, educational, or business use. Please contact your local bookseller or the Macmillan Corporate and Premium Sales Department at 1-800-221-7945, extension 5442, or by email at MacmillanSpecialMarkets@macmillan.com.

First Edition: 2025

This edition was printed by Bertelsmann Printing Group.

10   9   8   7   6   5   4   3   2   1

I dedicate this book to my daughter, Ava, who is my life force . . . my everything, my only thing, my number one.

A significant moment in my life that made me proud was when my dad was driving and picked me up from school.

I chose this because my dad got in a terrible accident where he got run over by a snowcat. I got to see him get better over time and it's made me so proud of how strong he is. When Friday came around each week, I would always be so excited to go to my dad's house and see my entire family. One Friday, my grandma, Meemaw, was picking me up from school, or that was what I thought. As I get called on the speaker, I walked over, super-excited to go home and see my dad. The last weekend I saw him, he was in his wheelchair. As I walked over to the car, I saw my dad was driving! I couldn't believe at first, but then also wasn't surprised. I knew always since I was a little kid, he was the strongest, most powerful guy on earth. Not only is he strong, he is the sweetest, most funny guy alive. In the car on the way back home I was thinking how incredibly lucky I am to have an amazing, strong dad.

—Ava Renner, essay for school entitled
"The Most Significant Event That Made You Proud"

CONTENTS

AUTHOR'S NOTE

I did not want to write this book.

I did not want to relive, moment by moment, word by word, the events of January 1, 2023. I did not want to recount the incident and its violence, nor the ramifications—on me and everyone around me—that followed: the life and death, the pain, the surgeries, the fear, the difficult recovery.

Also, I did not want to write this book because I couldn't imagine why people would care about what happened on that driveway that morning.

But in recent months I've come to understand the ripple effect this incident has had, and continues to have, even as time has passed. Because what happened did not just happen to me.

So even though I'm not a writer, and didn't want to write a book, here it is.

MY NEXT BREATH

ONE SHOT

Not today, motherfucker . . ."

That's the last thing I remember shouting.

The snowcat was sliding across the ice toward Alex. Alex is my nephew; he's twenty-seven, my sister Kym's youngest. I've always had a kind of father-son relationship with him; he's one of the first boys in the extended family; very sweet kid. The snowcat is a 14,000-pound industrial snow-clearing machine that I use on my property up in the mountains north of Lake Tahoe. That machine was heading toward him, and he had nowhere to escape to. His back was up against a huge Ford Raptor F-150 truck, which was itself jammed up against a snowbank.

It was January 1, 2023.

I believe that the most important thing in life is to take action. Feel everything, consider everything, read, think, ponder, cogitate—all that's fine. But you have to *do* something; you have to commit to action whenever you can. Don't only *think* about things, don't just *feel* things—take the first step, and then the next, and then the next. Do it. Otherwise, nothing's going to change, nothing's going to get better for you or for the people around you. In the end, it doesn't actually matter what you think or how you feel . . . everyone is a mass of feelings and emotions—some good, some bad. But emotions never built a bridge or fed the hungry or saved a life. I mean, who cares how you feel? *Do* something.

An immense 14,000-pound machine was sliding toward my nephew; I had to *do* something; in those lightning-fast seconds, his life hung in the balance. If that machine was to hit him, it would have crushed him to death, no question. But this New Year was going to be the same as any previous year in one crucial way: To me, action was everything. It's at the core of who I am. I do stuff; I take action; I believe in the power of a deed done.

I am blessed by a large extended family whom I love more than anything; and I believe in action. These two immovable forces—love and action—were about to collide.

I had no choice. I had one shot.

One shot—a long shot, but a shot. Not for a second did I think about my other life, the one in which I do most of my own stunts, the Hawkeye I inhabit in movies. This man faced with one shot is not, at that moment, a Hollywood actor. He's just me, Jeremy Renner, uncle to Alex, father to Ava, son and brother and uncle—friend to many, pain in the ass to plenty—half a mile down his driveway from his home in Lake Tahoe, where right now, back up there at the house, folks are innocently getting ready for a ski trip after days being snowed in by a monster storm.

I live for that gang up at the house. They are my whole life, my heart. I love each one of them with such an intensity . . . but here, now, I had one thing to do: I had to save Alex.

One shot, one action that would change everything and come to define the second half of my life: a three-foot leap up and a nearly three-foot leap across to the cabin of the snowcat, where I would grab the door handle, get inside that cab, hit the big red STOP button sitting up on the center of the console. The snowcat is charging toward Alex. He's got no escape route. The snowcat weighs over 14,000 pounds. He's standing by an F-150, which is itself against a snowbank. He's going to be crushed between the Ford and the thick steel blades of the snowcat; he's got nowhere to go . . .

One shot.

"Not today, motherfucker . . ."

This all happened in milliseconds. In the time it takes to type "one shot," I had to make that leap. I didn't have time to compute distances, to prepare my bones, no time to loosen my muscles—my only hope in saving Alex is to jump three feet across, nearly three feet up, grab the door, hit the button. My eyes dart, my blood tenses, something in my stomach shifts to the very bottom, a mixture of dread and opportunity jangles my senses and makes me less human, more animal.

Animal takes over: Alex is my blood, and like a wild beast I have to get between him and death. This is no longer conscious thought. This is pure action, motivated by love.

I didn't have time to consider my options, if indeed there were any. I had one shot at that leap . . .

. . . and I missed.

And then everything changed forever.

PART ONE

INCIDENT

1

SNOWMAGGEDON

We really shouldn't have been in Lake Tahoe in the first place.

Every year, I bring my entire extended family up to my house a few miles northeast of the lake, where I host a big event to celebrate the New Year. Christmases in the Renner family tend to be spent apart—most of my siblings have their own kids, so they hunker down at home to celebrate—but New Year's is different. That's when as many of my family as possible come to Camp Renner, which is what I call my house in Tahoe, so we can have a week of skiing and snowboarding and food and celebration of the fluke of the calendar that means everyone gets a new start. Usually there are twenty-five to thirty of us, and this year, as with every year, I had been looking forward to getting together with everyone for months. In a busy life, filled with work and travel and thousands of distractions—the mundane business of being alive—this annual get-together served to remind me why I work so hard in the first place: I get to take a breath, on the top of a mountain, away from the pressures of success. I am blessed to have a home big enough to host as many people as can come.

But by the end of 2022 it seemed like everything was against it.

For a start, I managed to miss my flight . . . by just a few seconds. The morning of December 28 my daughter Ava and my nephew Alex were to travel with me from Burbank Airport in Los Angeles up to Reno. I'm usually pretty good at making flights, but that day we had a ton of luggage, and our two dogs, and there were always some last-minute things we needed that we'd have to check we packed, and anyway, even though we bucked it the thirty minutes from the Hollywood Hills, where I have a house, to the airport for our flight, we somehow managed to cut it too close. We were at the gate a full fifteen minutes before the flight was due to take off, and it's a small airport and a small airplane . . . It wasn't like we were taking an Airbus 380 to Singapore. We were all checked in, too—but as we arrived at the gate, the crew had just that second closed the cabin doors.

"Dude," I pleaded to the nearest attendant who had literally just finished calling our names into the loudspeaker, "let me squeeze on, please. We're here, you checked us in and everything."

"Sorry, sir," he said, "we can't open the door once it's closed. FAA regulations . . ."

No amount of pleading worked, and it wasn't as if we could wait for the next flight. Every other flight was fully booked, and there was a major storm heading to Tahoe; we were screwed. I was distraught—people had already started their own journeys from all points north, south, east, and west to head to Camp Renner, and I had ruined the holiday. There was nothing we could do now but take a car back to my house in Hollywood, get all the luggage and the dogs back into the house, and then decide what to do. Everything had been prepared to host twenty, twenty-five people, but now the host can't make it?

Back at the house, I just couldn't face giving up. It's time to do something; it's time to take action.

"Screw it. Alex," I said, "let's just drive up there. What is it, eight hours? The car's all-wheel if the weather gets really shitty. Let's do it."

We were up against time, the fading light—I really didn't want to drive in the dark—and the weather. But sometimes you just have to commit to an action and do it, so that's what we did. We packed up the car once again—Ava, Alex, dogs, luggage—and headed out. It had been a crazy day already, but I was feeling good about the decision; I recorded a video message to the rest of the family telling them our plan.

One last thing to do before we headed north: I pulled over into a gas station on Franklin and Highland in the heart of Hollywood, about three miles down the hill, and filled up.

Nothing could stop us now.

Wrong.

With the car full of gas, I hopped back into the driver's seat and hit the START button on the car.

Nothing.

I press it again.

Nothing.

I look at Alex, who looks at me. Is it the battery? Did I not put the gas cap back on properly?

And then it hits me.

"Alex," I said, very slowly as the information settled in my brain stem, "I put the key fob on the top of the car as we were leaving the house, and now I can't find it . . ."

Oh shit.

That fob could now be anywhere between my house and this gas station—three miles of busy LA roads. I have a car full of stuff, my daughter, Alex, two dogs, and a houseful of people waiting for me eight hours north of this crappy little gas station in Hollywood.

There's only one thing for it.

"Alex, we're going to have to wait here, and you're going to have to get an Uber back to the house," I said. "I bet the key fell off right as we left. There's no way it stayed on much farther than next to the property, right?"

Alex's face betrayed enough doubt that I don't think I fully believed he'd find the key fob, but I also felt like we'd had enough bad luck that day.

Ava and I waited as Alex headed back to the house. The dogs looked at me, confused, but then they're always confused, especially as one of them survived a coyote attack and subsequently and understandably identifies as a cat.

After about half an hour, an Uber pulled up into the gas station, and Alex jumped out, holding the fob triumphantly. Sure enough, it had fallen off pretty much as we left the property.

It was a Christmas miracle. Laughing, we set out, Ava hunkered down in the back, Alex my copilot.

The dogs set to snoring, though I swear one of them also meows. We head north up out of the city, and then we thrum to the familiar rhythm of towns along the Antelope Valley and the Sierra Nevadas: Palmdale, Lancaster, Mojave, Indian Wells, Lone Pine—where Mount Whitney, sharp and serene, jags up into the clear blue—then Big Pine, Bishop, Mammoth, South Lake Tahoe. The weather deteriorates, the night descends, but nothing was going to stop us.

We arrive as the last light leaves. When we'd left LA, it had been sixty-one degrees; now, up on Mount Rose where my house sits, it's twenty-nine. In a matter of hours, the storm will begin; it will be an epochal weather event.

There will be so much snow to clear.

*   *   *

Camp Renner sits 7,300 feet above sea level at the end of a long, winding driveway that climbs to an expansive parking area in front of the main house, and then another, smaller guesthouse farther up the hill. When you live that high in the Sierra Nevadas, you get used to snow, but that year we faced something extra. We'd already had a good dump of snow, but what was coming was going to be a generational storm on top of it—the forecasters were predicting record-breaking weather. The *Tahoe Daily Tribune* summed up the magnitude of the situation on December 30, 2022:

> The National Weather Service in Reno on Thursday upgraded to a winter storm warning that lasts through 4 a.m. Sunday, Jan. 1, for up to 5 feet of snow above 8,000 feet, 1 to 3 feet above 7,000 feet . . .
>
> An avalanche warning is in effect through 7 a.m. Sunday for the storm packing gale force winds and rain on snow followed by high intensity snowfall could result in large, widespread, destructive slides.
>
> Strong winds will gust up to 50 mph with 100 mph or more possible for Sierra ridges.
>
> Travel over mountain passes likely won't be impacted with snow until midday Saturday.

Five feet of snow—we get a lot up at Mount Rose, but even to us that sounded like a huge amount. No doubt we would lose power at some point, and in all likelihood, we'd be snowed in, too, but what we didn't want was to get snowed out before we even got there.

Alex and Ava and I had arrived ahead of the storm—just—and the rest of the family managed to make it, too (though not my mom—she was in our hometown of Modesto with my brother Kyle and Katie, his wife, who had just had their first child). Some friends were joining, too, and soon the house was bustling with people, sitting around in the kitchen catching up, playing pool by the big front window, the kids thick as thieves, hunkering down in the TV room.

Once the storm started it just never stopped. It was gorgeous to watch from the safety of the house. Slanting shards of snow rattled the great window, covering the cars and the snowmobiles, dulling all sounds until all we could hear was the soft buzzy call of the mountain chickadees and the urgent whistling of the western tanagers. After a few hours great globs of heavy wetness hung from the ponderosas and the sugar pines, looking for all the world like the fake stuff you spray on Christmas trees. By the time the New Year approached, the whole of western Nevada was buried under those epochal five feet, and one day stuck turned into two turned into three.

This is the best—and worst—thing about where I live. Each year we seem to get a stretch where the winds whip to one hundred miles per hour, huge snow amounts fall, and we're on avalanche—and lightning and tornado—watch. Power fails; roads close; ski-resort funiculars hang useless in the ice-bound air. The National Weather Service sends out warnings with homey phrases like, "Best to hunker down where you are," but when all the roads are closed and the power goes out, there's really no choice: it can be treacherous to be a human in the face of all this nature. And yet the extraordinary beauty and opportunities for adventure that the snow affords make living in the mountains a true privilege.

By the last day of 2022 we had no cell service and no internet, meaning no phones, no tablets, no TVs. The kids had long given up the TV room to come and hang out with the adults. We were just one big extended happy family, no longer separated by the glow of screens—what a marvel that was in and of itself.

I didn't mind at all that we were snowed in—I'm always prepared for that kind of thing. You have to be at 7,300 feet in Nevada.

In another life I inhabited Staff Sergeant William James in *The Hurt Locker* and Hawkeye in *The Avengers* and my current gig playing the lead in *Mayor of Kingstown*, but that's what I do for a living. Much more importantly, I am simply Jeremy, father to Ava, my magical, perfect daughter; I am Jeremy, the proud brother of Kym, my brilliant, beautiful sister, and doting uncle to her kids, Alex and his sisters Kayla and Bella; I am brother to Kyle, who had just had his baby. I'm the son of a strong, inspirational mom—Valerie Cearley to some but Meemaw to most who know her well, who was right then with her new grandson a few hours away in Modesto, where we grew up. I am the son of a dreamer, intellectual father, Lee Renner, who had once run the McHenry Bowl in Modesto before becoming a college guidance counselor. I was proud brother to my other siblings, Clayton and Arthur and Theo and Nicky, and benevolent (I hope!) brother-in-law and uncle to their various partners and kids.

Like all families since the dawn of time, we'd been through some shit, but we loved nothing more than getting together to celebrate holidays, whether it was July 4 or New Year's. And through it all I've never lost sight of the *normal* life; maybe coming into the peak of my career a little later than some, in my thirties and after, helped me keep my feet on the ground? Whatever it was, I never needed reminding that I was a lucky man to have so many people to love and who loved me.

That New Year's felt extra special to me; I don't know why. Perhaps it was because we were so snowed in; perhaps it was that I knew everyone had had to try so hard to get to Camp Renner in the first place, given that it's isolated and the weather was so lousy. Perhaps it was just the passage of years deepening my already strong bond with these amazing people, especially as it became increasingly hard to fight against the constraints of my job, which both gave me so many opportunities and benefits but also squeezed me for time. Or maybe it was a throwback: no phones, no TVs, no distractions except for raucous games of pool lit by strings of Christmas lights hooked up to the generator.

I can't put my finger on exactly why, but I loved those few days so much; we got to play silly games and have real conversations and truly connect away from social media and email and doomscrolling.

My niece Kayla told me later that she'd had a private talk with her partner, Mark, during that week.

"Jeremy is interacting with us in ways that I'd never seen before," she told him. "He is being incredibly intentional in every conversation and so physically close, too. Have you noticed how he's holding intense eye contact, constantly telling us how much he loves us?"

Mark agreed—he'd noticed my behavior, too.

It's true; I was intensely grateful to have my family there that year. I'm always happy they come, but something about braving that dangerous weather to spend time together felt like a beautiful expression of our shared love. And despite my job as an actor and despite how much time I spend in front of people, I can still be quite an interior person; a stranger meeting me might think of me as wary, shy, or standoffish, or a combination of all three. In large group settings I'll often be the one escaping out back to have a cigarette, slipping away when no one's looking. This is not because I don't love my family; rather it's because I've always been quite private, and I value whatever time I can get to step back from life and think about things. My father taught me to be analytical, and from childhood I was quite happy to be solitary. Now, in adulthood, I often found myself on the edge of a crowd, looking out into the dark of the snowbound yard as much as I looked back into the warmth of the house.

I'm not surprised Kayla and Mark saw a difference in me those few days. I didn't plan on being more engaged than usual, it just felt natural.

As we welcomed in the New Year, I couldn't help but take a moment to let gratitude fill me, as the love of this huge family filled me, too. Even if we couldn't charge our phones or watch movies, we could just sit around, shooting the shit, and though we were snowed in, there was a magic to it that only a family can understand. The kids were running back and forth, like tides, this way and that, chasing each other, once in a while falling out with each other, then just as quickly laughing again; Kym would suddenly and magically rustle up a delicious spaghetti Bolognese or a roast; Alex and I would discuss whether or not my beloved San Francisco 49ers would beat the Las Vegas Raiders on New Year's Day, and how far we thought our team could go in the playoffs.

Now and then, Ava would take a break from running around with her cousins and come and hang out with me on the couch.

"Daddy," she said, "how long do you think we'll be snowed in?"

"Not much longer," I said, "and when we *do* get out, we're going to ski our butts off."

My daughter and I have always had a very mature relationship—as her teen years approached people liked to tease me that she was going to be a terror, but I always pushed back.

"My daughter has too much accountability, too much responsibility to life and everything around her to be like that," I'd say, and so far, I was right about that.

Ava is my all.

*   *   *

It's not easy feeding twenty-five people with no power.

My sister Kym is a really good cook, and bless her, she decided to cook a roast, but it became the longest roast ever cooked—and, in her own words, "the grossest." Over and over the power would go out, and she'd have to plug the stove into the generator, but then that would stop working, and she'd have to wait, then restart the roasting, all the time leaving the meat sitting around in what amounted to what she called "fatty waters." (That's as appetizing as it sounds.) It wasn't her fault, but neither was it cordon bleu—it was more like cordon beige by the time it was finished, and with the best will in the world it wasn't the most enticing piece of meat anyone had ever seen. It was absolutely typical of her to try to feed everyone something delicious, but the power situation meant that she was fighting a losing battle from minute one right through minute one thousand.

It was New Year's Eve by this point, and we needed food. Though the kids were having a great time, I knew we'd need to get something on the table to distract them from the dead roast and to help them stay up for midnight, so I decided to head down to Reno—usually about a twenty-minute drive—to get pizzas for everyone before the roads finally closed. Given the extent of the storm I wasn't even sure I'd make it, but I couldn't just sit around and wonder.

It was time to *do*.

I took my pal Rory Millikin with me.

Rory is a larger-than-life Canadian who's so approachable and goofy-funny that the kids take it in turns running past him to knock his baseball cap off (but only when he's sitting down—when he's standing, he's six foot five). He's also my partner in our RennerVation project—together we acquire and rehabilitate old trucks, ambulances, buses, and other large, decommissioned vehicles, repurpose them sometimes, and then donate them to communities that need them. We'd recently finished filming a first season of documentaries about the project, *Renner-vations*, for Disney. In the series we turned a tour bus into a mobile music studio in Chicago; a city bus into a dance studio for people living at the southern tip of Baja, Mexico; a shuttle bus into a rec center for Reno; and even created a mobile water treatment bus for folks in Rajasthan, India. The producers had initially been skeptical of Rory's involvement because they didn't exactly know who he was, but then they met him and realized, like we all did, that his charisma was off the charts and invaluable in making mountains move to his will (even if some of his efforts at actual renovations were what can only be described as not quite professional standard). No matter—Rory was integral to the show, as he was to my life as a friend, and we couldn't wait for the world to see the shows in the New Year.

Our friendship didn't start out too well, though. Rory is the proud son of a legendary political figure in Canada—Rory's father, Cameron Millikin, was originally from Ireland but once he immigrated to Canada it became part of his life's work to toil tirelessly for peace (he often played intermediary between the warring factions in Northern Ireland, and back home Cameron was also a close adviser to multiple Canadian prime ministers). Rory inherited his father's height (his dad was six foot seven), his charisma and powers of persuasion, and his almost perfect inability to recognize people. Daddy Millikin was infamous for not knowing who Julia Roberts and Denzel Washington were when he bumped into them in a hotel in London (he reportedly told them both that they should consider having a backup plan because acting is a tough gig), and he once even turned away Ronnie Wood of the Rolling Stones from his front door, assuming he was a homeless guy begging for a handout (he was actually friends with Rory's brother).

So, true to the Millikin bloodline, the day I met Rory, he had no idea who I was, either. I had my head buried in my phone one evening at my house in Los Angeles when Rory had arrived with a mutual friend. He immediately started into gushing about a movie he'd just seen, *Arrival*. Turns out Rory loves science fiction and alien movies, but crucially he'd never seen an *Avengers* movie, or anything else I'd been in.

But it was nice to hear that this very tall stranger liked *Arrival*, so looking up briefly I said, "That movie was a lot of work . . ."

Rory looked quizzically at me.

"Well, not really," he said. "You just go online, get a ticket, and head to your nearest cinema . . ."

What now?

"No, no," I said. "I mean it took about six months."

"Wow, I'm from Canada, and I know that things are slower there," Rory said, "but even I just went to the movie theater one afternoon. The place was pretty full, but there were still seats available."

Bemused by the non sequitur about Canada, and realizing I'd only been half engaging at this point, now I properly looked up from my phone and squinted at this guy. Who *is* this towering idiot in my house?

"No," I said, trying again. "I was part of the movie."

"Oh," Rory said, "were you a lighting guy or something?"

I didn't like to point out that we were sitting in a big house in a secluded part of the Hollywood Hills . . . but clearly the penny wasn't dropping.

"I was one of the costars of the movie," I said, reluctantly. No actor even wants to have to say those words.

"Don't bullshit a bullshit artist," Rory said, as he reached over to remove my glasses and baseball cap to get a better look at me. (No, he really did that.) And then he was inches away from my face, peering at me like a crime victim trying to memorize every inch of their assailant for a subsequent police lineup.

"No, you were *not*," Rory said, definitively. "I *just* saw the movie. *Definitely not you!*"

Then he tried to put my glasses back on my face but managed only to poke me in the eye with one of the stems.

I really didn't know what else to say. Plus, now my eye was watering.

"I was the *physicist*," I said, trying to remain calm. "You know, the guy in the scene when the heptapod thing comes up to the wall?"

This seemed to ring a bell for Rory, but still he seemed dubious. And then I did something I never usually do.

"Give me your phone," I said. Rory handed me his iPhone and I went straight to his contacts and added my name and number.

"Text me," I said. "You'll find it under 'Jeremy Renner.' And tomorrow morning, once you've texted me, I'll either invite you back here to grill and hang out, or I will have already changed my mind, and I will block you and delete your number forever."

Honestly at that point it could have gone either way. This giant of a man had just told me I wasn't in a movie I knew I was in because I'd been in it, and, in arguing the point, had also managed to almost poke my eye out with my own reading glasses. Also, did I mention he kept mentioning he was Canadian?

To this day I'm not sure why, but the next morning I texted Rory and he came back to my house that day to hang out.

We've been pretty much inseparable ever since, so it was natural that New Year's Eve that he'd ride shotgun with me in my Ford Raptor to the Walmart in nearby Reno to pick up some wood and other supplies, and those crucial pizzas. But the weather was deteriorating even then, and though we got down the mountain just about okay, we almost didn't make it back. We were only gone for an hour, but by the time we neared home, with a sinking heart we saw that the mountain was now closed. On Mount Rose Highway, just a mile or two from my house, I found a roadblock in place, flashing blue lights, the whole nine.

An NDOT guy ambled over to my truck as I wound down my window.

"I'm heading up to my house—"

He interrupted me.

"We can't let you. The police chief said to close the highway," he said, and then turned to walk away.

"Come on, man, you're kidding," I said, "it's fucking New Year's Eve."

The NDOT guy stopped, then turned back. This could go either way, especially as I'd dropped the f-bomb in my F-150.

"No can do," he said, evenly.

"Dude," I said, "I went down *five* minutes to get some food. You can't not let me up to my house. I have twenty-five people up there with no power, including a bunch of kids, and they're hungry."

"Highway's closed," he said, a bit more sternly. "We're just doing what we're told. I'm not losing my job over this."

"I get it, man, I truly do, but I drive this shit all the time, dude . . . you know I live up there . . ." But before I could plead anymore, he was already halfway back to the warmth of his truck.

I didn't take this well; there were a bunch of little kids, and their adults, who needed me. I was getting up there one way or the other.

Family is everything to me; maybe I didn't know that day quite how much (though the universe was about to send me a lesson on that one). I wasn't about to let a closed mountain stop my getting back to them.

Rory was fine, by the way—he was already working his way through one of the pizzas.

"Thank fucking God we got pizza," he said, laughing.

"We're blocked from going back up the hill," I said, "there are twenty-five people hungry and without power, and we could be here at this road-block for days, but at least you've decided to not go hungry."

And with that, I pulled out a piece of pizza, too. Then, I set about calling everybody I knew in Reno; I couldn't just sit there forever eating pizza. I started with my friend Jesse, a former firefighter, who just happened to be hanging with the local chief of police that night. Jesse told me the only way I was getting back to my house was if I agreed to be escorted up the mountain; it took an hour for the escort to arrive, and let's just say I wasn't in the best mood by that point, though I'd managed to stop Rory from eating *all* the food. But in fairness, the escort was great;

knowing the roads like I did, in the end I basically escorted him up, even urging him to leave me at the foot of my driveway given that it was still a half mile to my house. He wouldn't take no for an answer, and though he was a really solid driver, in the end the weather was so bad I had to haul him out of a snowbank so he could head back down the hill.

All good; we had made it home, and there was even some pizza left—we had everything we needed to celebrate the coming New Year together. Everything was picture perfect; the snow was creeping up the windowpanes; the fairy lights strung across the pool table etched an eerie glow across all of our excited faces; at midnight, we managed to get enough service to watch the ball drop on a cell phone, though it was about 3:03 by the time we finally got the picture clear enough to see (we were three hours behind New York, of course). There was Times Square from three hours earlier, crazy with crowds and kissing, and there we were, three thousand miles to the west, one great happy family snowed in amid the silence of a mountain hideaway.

As the clock struck midnight, or whatever time it actually was, as yet more snow fell, we toasted our good fortune, another year successfully navigated. I was blessed to be with my family first and foremost, but beyond that, I was lucky enough to be able to make films, movies that brought me the blessed chance to own a magical property in the mountains above Lake Tahoe (even if dolts like Millikin didn't recognize me), the chance to tell stories that mattered, that meant something to so many people. But at heart, in the deepest places of me, I was just Jeremy, one part of the Renner family, a family that loved each other and cared for each other and more than anything just wanted to spend time together whenever we could.

The year 2023 was going to be a great one. There were more movies to make, more TV shows to film, the *Rennervations* series on Disney+, more old ambulances and fire trucks to buy to repurpose for people. I was sometimes too busy to do the things I really wanted to do, which mainly revolved around spending time with Ava. My work could take me away from her all too much, and it could make me frustrated and dissatisfied with life. I missed her first birthday because I'd been filming *Mission: Impossible—Ghost Protocol* in London. I'd been miserable over there—all I wanted to do was to see her, to be around her. And after that I told myself that from then on I would make different decisions: I was now loath to ever work out of the country because it was imperative for me that she got to see my face every night before she went to bed and every morning when she awoke.

But any thoughts of a storm in my career, like the storm outside, would surely pass; New Year morning's forecast was for sun-dazzled, sharp skies, a picture postcard of a perfect winter scene, 7,300 feet up in the Tahoe air. Yes, the storm was passing, if only briefly, but I already knew that when the sun hit the snow-heavy pines at dawn, the landscape would transform from magical to unforgettable. Yes, we were snowed in and playing pool by fairy lights, but none of it mattered. True, the buildings farther up the property, where the heavy-duty snow blowers were housed, were fully snowed in, but we'd need something more heavy-duty to shift five feet of snow in any case.

Fortunately, I own a snowcat.

Snowcats (the name is a mix of "snow" and "cat," for "caterpillar") are industrial snow removers, invaluable in ski resorts (my model is a 1988 PistenBully, #901, the brand name a pun on the word "piste"). These things are so powerful, tanklike, yet they basically float over the snow. The machine's central, bright-orange cab sits up above two sets of galvanized steel tracks that extend outward a couple of feet beyond the body of the vehicle, driven as they are by six heavy wheels on each side. In front, a massive metal shovel lies the entire width of the machine, big enough to deal with the depths of snow that falls on mountains. In fact, the snowcat is so big that when you're in the cab, it's hard to see what's in front of you—you're up so high that you could easily run over a car in a drift before you even knew it was there.

I'd owned the PistenBully for a few years—in fact, it conveyed with the house when I bought it. After all these winters of plowing the house out all the way to the road, I could maneuver the snowcat like a pro, though it's not a particularly complicated machine in the first place. Basically, you start it up, press the accelerator, and then, to stop it, you stop pressing the gas before engaging the main hand brake—and to stop the engine, cunningly enough you hit the button that reads STOP. Without the snowcat, there could be no way I'd be able to live at the top of a half-mile driveway at 7,300 feet when it's covered in nearly 150 inches of powder. I would usually rev up the PistenBully each day to keep up with the snowfall, clearing two or three feet at a time, but this storm had been so fast and so intense, there was no way to make a dent in the drifts until the storm relented.

But the real snow removal could wait for the morning. Now, everyone was heading out into the driveway to have a huge snowball fight. Kayla later said she hadn't played like that since she'd been a little kid. "It was a celebration of life," she told me later, "playful, easy. It's almost like you had set the tone by being so open and loving." I watched them all out there, hurling snow at each other, tackling each other down into the powder. I wish my mom had been there—she and Kym had been on the outs for almost six months, which was the longest anyone in our family had ever gone without talking. I hoped the new year would bring a resolution to the argument; I was sure it would. It was a rarity for this kind of thing to happen in the Renner family, and we usually always found a way to fix whatever ailed us.

There is so much love in our family. We'd clear away the pain like so much snow, I was sure of it.

My pal Dave Kelsey and I, along with Rory and Alex, would wake up early in the morning and start a real cleanup of the snow. And then, if the nearby ski mountain was open—and doing our best to ignore the cognitive dissonance that even though we figured nobody would make it up the mountain the next day, they'd still open up the mountain *just for us*—we'd load up the kids and snowboards and skis and head up the half mile to the highway and the nearby slopes, and on into a new year filled with hope, excitement, and even more gratitude.

Everything was as close to perfect as you could get. It was such a special night at the end of a special few days. I was with the people I love the most, we had made it to Camp Renner, we were together, and tomorrow? Maybe we could get out finally, get down some ski runs, whooping at the promise of another year to cherish.

We were safe, cocooned, happy; this was the typical Renner New Year. And if the weather got gnarly again, and we really wanted to escape, we always had the snowcat.

2

SNOWCAT

- ○ Always take a firm grip on grab handle of the driver's door when entering the vehicle.
- ○ Step onto the track.
- ○ Risk of slipping on the track when climbing into and out of driver's cab. Always take a firm grip on the handle in order to step onto the track . . .
- ○ Always take a firm grip on grab handle of the driver's door.
- ○ Fully raise armrest.
- ○ Take a grip on steering wheel and swing yourself into the driver's seat.
- ○ Close the door.

—EXCERPT FROM A PISTENBULLY USER MANUAL

At around six a.m., New Year's Day, 2023, I jump up into the snowcat and get to work.

The forecast had called for a break in the storm, a break that would last long enough to clear the driveway and would also extend into the rest of the day so we could finally get off the property. But to shift this much snow, and to unbury snowmobiles and vehicles ahead of any escape, I am going to need help, so I send Rory to wake up Alex. Rory's efforts don't take the first time—Alex had had a few adult beverages the night before and had gotten to bed later than most, so when Rory tries to rouse him, he's not really having it. The second time Alex relents and comes out to join Rory, Dave, and me.

Dave Kelsey is a longtime friend of mine, from acting class in our twenties. Back then we'd both been struggling actors but eventually did a really funny movie together called *Fish in a Barrel*. All these years later we were still close friends, and our kids were close, too, so it was natural that he and his family would be with us for New Year's. Now the four of us—Rory, Dave, Alex, and I—are out in the predawn, embarking on what would probably be a few hours of snow removal.

I fire up the cat; Dave asks if I want him to work it, but I tell him I got it. Instead, he starts digging out some snowmobiles, but it is tough going. As we work, Dave and I sometimes pause to talk and to take in the scene. It is around seven thirty a.m. by this point, the most beautiful morning you could imagine.

"Man," Dave says, "what an incredible night. That was the best New Year's I think I've ever had." I agree. We chat about how grateful we both are for our lives, for our families, for each other, and for this moment, which just then feels like a kind of heaven on earth. The sun isn't quite yet up, and the quiet is breathtaking, made even more profound by the snow cover, a peace pierced only by the Steller's jays squawking through the still air. The mountain is still closed, no vehicles racing the curves down on the Mount Rose Highway; Dave and I share that moment, side by side, facing into a new year together as we had so many times; but this one did indeed feel even more significant and hopeful than usual. And yes, we still believed they'd open the slopes just for us . . .

Eventually we get back to work. Getting the snowmobiles unstuck is a heavy toil, though—the only way forward is to dig out individual machines, and even then, it's easy to get them re-stuck in snowdrifts.

Initially Alex had been dubious that we were getting off the property at all that day. He was right to point out that below the fresh powder there was a bunch of really iced-up snow that had been sitting there for two or three days, but still we had to try. Still, as we begin to dig stuff out, Alex isn't having it.

"This is fucking stupid, Rory," he says.

"A Train," Rory says, using his nickname for Alex (A Train equals "cool," or something—you'd have to ask Rory), "shut the fuck up, dude." Rory didn't help his case with Alex by whistling and being annoyingly jovial, either.

"We're not going anywhere, guys," Alex tries again. "This is a waste of time. Look at the road. There are still cars broken down."

Sure enough, out on the Mount Rose Highway, as daylight arrives, we can make out abandoned vehicles up and down the hill. Still, we've been snowed in for days, and it's time to make a break for it. No one really wants to listen to what Alex has to say, though he's probably right. He, in turn, realizing he is losing the argument, heads back into the house to get the keys to a storage facility we keep a quarter of a mile down the hill so he can get a snowmobile and bring it back up. What should have taken him five minutes takes thirty because of the snowdrifts he has to wade through, and once he reaches the storage units, he can't get in anyway— either he's brought the wrong key or the lock is frozen, so he has to trudge back through those sixty inches of snow.

By the time he gets back I have the snowcat out on the driveway— Rory and David have gone back into the house to start breakfast and make coffee. Alex joins them, and by the time he comes back out, I've done one pass with the snowcat, but there is still so much snow to move.

It is time for plan B: I'll take the Raptor and try to muscle my way to the main road (which had been plowed by now)—at least then I'd know if I was able to make a path through, so we'd be able to get off the property that morning. If I could get the Raptor out, then we could load up people and head to the mountain to go skiing.

I head down the driveway in the Ford. It's going well, but then I reach a switchback—almost to the main road there's a subtle right turn after a left—and you have to turn the vehicle ever so slightly so as not to fall over the edge, but the Raptor just starts to slip and slide before heading straight into a snowbank.

Fuck, what do we do now? Alex is farther up the driveway, and I watch as he looks at the snowcat. I can see he's considering bringing it down to help. I know he's never actually driven it, but I also know he's good with vehicles and he can just figure it out. There are levers for the front blade, but beyond pressing gas and not pressing gas, it's not a complicated machine to drive.

As the PistenBully operating manual describes it, to get into the cab you have to climb on the galvanized steel tracks, grab the driver's door handle, and hoist yourself up into the driver's seat—in all, it's about three feet up and three across the tracks from the ground to the door. I watch as Alex hops up and starts to maneuver the machine down the driveway.

Once he arrives, we switch places—I go up into the cab of the snowcat, and Alex jumps down and attaches the Ford to the back of the snowcat with chains, and we get to pulling the F-150 out.

I've cleared most of the snow—all that's left is a thick layer of ice and the asphalt of the driveway. We get the truck unstuck, and Alex goes to unlatch it from the snowcat. I start to turn the snowcat around, but its huge snow blade is up high, and I can't quite see Alex in front of me. As I'm trying to work out if he's clear, the ice causes the snowcat to skid a little, backing it up for a second, so the only way to get a view of what's happening is to momentarily step onto the galvanized steel tracks—there's no platform, nothing, just the steel. I get out of the driver's seat, and step on the tracks to talk to Alex.

Per the manual:

- **Before exiting the driver's cab!—Apply parking brake**

I don't engage the parking brake, or disengage the steel tracks.

In that moment—an innocent, critical, life-changing moment—when I didn't set the parking brake, this tiny, monumental slip of the mind would change the course of my life forever, and of so many other lives, too. Nothing after that moment could yet be imagined.

The snowcat begins to slide on the icy asphalt toward Alex, and I realize with a horror that he's in danger. He is on the ground handling the hooks and heavy chains as the menacing cat inches toward him. I step back in the cab and press the reverse toggle switch on the steering column briefly to back up and to give him a few more feet of room. I put the toggle back in park. I step out halfway once again to discuss our next steps. Alex is out of sight, still working on the ground, I assume, so I shout something over the rumble of the noisy diesel engine. But I am interrupted by the loud scraping metal as the snowcat slips across the ice again. I am off balance and my hand accidentally hits the toggle forward, throwing me backward, off toward the snowbank.

The snowcat is now charging in its forward gear toward Alex, who is doomed to be crushed between the snow blade and the F-150, which sits perpendicular to the snowcat only ten or twelve feet away.

Time slows to a near stop for me, even as it hurries through each brief second like a thunderclap. I hear the cracking of the ice under the tracks of the snowcat, the lumbering torque of the engine, unfeeling and monotonous. There is a heaviness to the motion of the machine that is otherworldly; it brings with it an authority, a weight, an unyielding purpose, monstrous. It is the unstoppable force, but I realize with a shock—coming back into real time in a flash, a millisecond—that Alex is the immovable object.

He is no match for a 14,000-pound beast.

Somehow, I have to stop the snowcat.

Per the manual:

- ○ **If you hit the STOP button, the PistenBully brakes sharply to a complete stop.**
- ○ **Hit the STOP button in the event of sudden danger.**

I have one shot—a leap up and across the snowcat's metal tracks, back into the cab, where hopefully I can hit the STOP button.

"Not today, motherfucker," I shout. My nephew is about to be crushed to death; this cannot happen. All my years of taking action, of loving my family, have led to this moment in time, this unspoken, blood-deep New Year's resolution to do everything I can to save Alex from a terrible fate. It's not even as if I have a conscious thought—I'm all instinctual, animal movement, synapses firing in perfect coordination with a heart filled with love for this young man, for all my family.

It's as simple and as profound as that.

All the other elements of this: the snow, the new year, the F-150, the fucking parking brake. None of them matters.

I make the leap. In retrospect it's an impossible thing to have attempted— to jump across three feet of spinning tracks as the machine slides forward, up into a cab where my only option was to slam my fist into a red STOP button. But love doesn't wait for the impossible, doesn't countenance doubt or nonaction, at least not for me. If you have one shot, you have one shot, and you have to take it.

It wasn't as if I had a choice.

The only way to measure progress is to know where you started from. That split-second moment, that leap, that one shot, was where I started. It was an act entirely motivated by love, by family, by an innate sense of "rather me than him, rather me than anyone."

But love would have to wait to save me, because in the immediate, my feet lose their grip on the moving tracks, and I never make it to the cab.

What happens, from leap to the end of the incident, takes place across perhaps ten seconds. I don't even remember if I did get close enough to make a grab for the cab door, though I probably didn't get close.

It doesn't matter now.

Unbound to the earth, unmoored from the machine momentarily, I lurch violently forward, out of control now. In that split second I am catapulted forward, off the spinning metal tracks, arms flailing, at the inexorable behest of gravity and kinetic energy, a man falling, grasping for nothing because there is nothing to grab on to, mid-disaster, a new chapter of his life beginning in the tumbling body he inhabits, as I arc over the front of the tracks, propelled forward by forces inexplicable and absolute, down onto the hard-packed ice, where my head hits the ground hard and instantly gashes open.

I'd missed my one shot. The snowcat continues to charge forward, only now I'm in the way of its huge steel tracks.

All thoughts of Alex, all thoughts of Ava, and Kym, and my mom, and the mountains, of movies and friends, the earth on which we spin, and everything in between . . . all thoughts of the life I once had are momentarily obliterated by the crack of my head, the disorientation of the violent fall, and the slow, steady, pulverizing momentum of this machine.

Already a huge crack to the head, gashing it, as I hit the iced asphalt. This injury might be enough for one day. But there is so much more.

The machine rumbles on, oblivious to me in its way. It is a monster without a soul, an automaton that cares nothing for humanity or life or body or soul.

There come terrible crunching sounds as 14,000 pounds of galvanized steel machinery slowly, inexorably, monotonously grinds over my body.

To this day, sometimes when I'm trying to sleep, I'll get an image popping into my brain. I'm at a drive-in theater: A car is late for the movie, you hear the tires rolling over the gravel, or else some other mystical vehicle with metal wheels is heard to grind over glass or pebbles. Imagine the crunching and cracking of rock and concrete under unfathomable heavy wheels. In our garage as a kid, I had a vise I'd put my skis in to tune them up and apply wax. Sometimes, though, when I was bored or curious, I would put a random object in the jaws of the vise and just crank that thing, just keep cranking it until whatever was in the vise started to fail: because that vise ain't losing, and I was fascinated by the uncompromising power of the absolute.

And that's what my skull sounded like: something losing out against the unmitigated power of power itself.

I can promise you this much at least: The sounds of being crushed are just as terrifying as the visual; perhaps more so. It is a horrifying soundtrack.

The reality of what is happening kicks in. I am holding my breath, and blood is rushing to my face, and I feel a super intense lightheadedness. And yet I am completely conscious of what is happening. I know I am under the machine. I have zero control. I know that my skull has split like a watermelon, my brain pulverized like meat.

It's so heavy.

I can't get away.

I have zero control.

No, no, no, no, no, no, no.

Legs and body instantly crushed, mangled, but I barely notice.

There are six sets of wheels on the machine, covered as they are by a corrugated track of seventy-six steel, teardrop-shaped ridges, each sharp end of which takes its turn to dig into my body, which lies between them and the ice-sharp asphalt. Skull, jaw, cheekbones, molars: all give way. The pressure repeats: skull, jawbone, cheek, molars giving way repeatedly. It felt just as you would imagine: force, pressure, release; force, pressure, release. Each wheel passing over me intensifies what is already unbearable, repetitive pressure, then a brief respite, then another wheel, and always those teardrop-shaped tracks, grinding me into the asphalt.

Six fucking wheels, seventy-six steel blades, 14,000 pounds of machine, all ranged against one human body. Skull, jaw, cheekbones, molars: fibula, tibia, lungs, eye sockets, cranium, pelvis, ulna, legs, arms, skin, crack, snap, crack, squeeze, crack.

More sounds: A ringing in the ears, as if a large-caliber gun has unloaded next to my head. A sting of bright white in my eyes—I am blinded by a coruscating lightning, a lightning that signals the break of my orbital bone, causing my left eyeball to violently burst out of my skull.

Fact: I can see my left eye with my right eye.

I am in thrall to the purified pressure of an unrelenting force meeting me, an immovable object.

I hear all the bones crack, every one of them. (I'll find out later that there are thirty-eight, maybe more, in various states of crack and shatter and twist and shard.)

Then, perhaps five seconds later, the machine has passed. My crushed body is relieved from the immense weight at last.

Go back and count five seconds.

One one thousand.

Two one thousand.

Three one thousand.

Four one thousand.

Five one thousand.

In each of those seconds, a man is pinned beneath 14,000 pounds of machinery, the pressure intensifying with each wheel, then lessening very slightly until the next wheel arrives. (There are six wheels in five seconds.) His bones are pulverized, his head cracked, his eyes reimagining their relationship to the skull, his lungs eviscerating. The machine is an unimaginable force delivered to the earth via brutalizing steel tracks and six wheels, but I don't need to imagine it.

I was that man. I am that man. I'll die that man.

*   *   *

From Alex's perspective, he told me later he watched as I turned the snowcat around, opened the door of the machine, and I yelled something.

"We're going to go . . ." he thinks I said, or something like it.

Then I jumped off the snowcat, but he can see it's moving. He heard me shout something, almost like a scream.

It was, "Not today, motherfucker."

Alex said he really didn't know what was happening.

Realizing with horror that the snowcat is coming for him, though genuinely not understanding why the snowcat was heading his way, Alex managed to quickly jump back into the Raptor, but he didn't even have time to close the door.

"Oh fuck, look at this thing," Alex said. In the truck now, he slammed it into reverse, hammering the gas, never taking his eyes off of the snowcat, hoping to escape the oncoming, and probably devastating, collision.

The Raptor door was open.

Alex says he closed his eyes.

Later he told me that his only thought as the snowcat approached was "Please be quick."

In fact, he said that phrase out loud, too, four or five times. "Please be quick. Please be quick. Please be quick. Please be quick. Please be quick."

He knew he was going to be crushed to death. Please be quick. Please be quick. Please be quick. Please be quick. Please be quick. I can't imagine the horror of that, and in retrospect it underlines my need to act, though I can't hear him, because I'm in an entirely different world of danger.

*   *   *

The machine has passed. I am face down in the ice.

I believe information is the key to avoiding one's fears.

I do not have the information to understand precisely what has happened.

I have no information about what state my bones are in, my body is in, only that a great disaster has befallen it.

Instead, I have only mute disbelief, a retreat from intelligence, animal shock, and this, my inexplicable new reality.

It may be true that I blacked out for a few seconds; I really can't say. The part of my brain that might accommodate the inputting of information is erased over, like a mockingbird's brain relearning and relearning its song. So many bones are broken. A gash in my head pours bright fresh blood all over the ice and asphalt.

My left eye is no longer held fast by my orbital bone.

Let's say I passed out briefly. It doesn't matter. Beyond all this, something even more fundamental is now in play.

What matters is, I'm not breathing.

I'm not breathing because I cannot breathe. I try, but the ordinary, instinctual, unthinking respiration I've taken for granted is now gone. I know it's a problem because if you have to try to breathe, this usually means you cannot breathe.

I cannot breathe. I am suffocating.

I need to head out on a quest to find the most fundamental thing to life: my next breath.

I have always been very conscious about my breathing. I once had placards on my wall in my apartment that I had engraved, "Don't forget to breathe." Whenever I opened my flip phone back then, the first thing I saw was the same message I'd typed into the home screen: "Don't forget to breathe." Breathing was my great anti-stressor. When I was nervous for an audition, I'd take controlled breaths while visualizing something grounded, like a tree in the earth. We all go through stuff in our lives that triggers us, that makes us miserable, pisses us off, makes us sad—and to combat these things, I've found myself using conscious breath. I don't need Valium; I need a deep breath, or several, or ten minutes of it; I don't need the hit from a joint: just breathe. It's so much better to trust your lungs than a drug. And with breathing you cement your relationship with your body because the breathing fixes the pain. It works.

All this I brought to that moment.

*   *   *

Given how bad this situation was, it seems churlish to imagine a worst-case scenario, but just for a moment, imagine if the snowcat hadn't passed over me in five seconds. Imagine if it had hit the Raptor and stalled instead of pushing the Ford truck farther into the snowbank—which is what happened—those medieval steel tracks, those six spinning wheels, those seventy-six steel blades, that 14,000 pounds of machine, would have continued their spin in place, pulverizing me endlessly and turning my body into little more than ground meat. Among the many miracles, thank God the snowcat had enough distance to keep going, to push that F-150, pushing it, in fact, sideways and into the snowbank. Because I was still under the tracks when the snowcat hit the Raptor, but nothing stopped its forward momentum, at least long enough for my body to be left clear and shattered on the icy driveway.

The beast was off me. In those seconds in which I may have initially passed out, the snowcat continued its agonizing march. For all my efforts, I have not stopped it; my shout of "Not today, motherfucker" hangs like a cruel admonition in the sharp January air. As the great weight of the machine rumbled on, it finally hits the Raptor, the immense blade of the snowcat closing the door tight. Alex has escaped by the slimmest of seconds—the snowcat pushes Alex and the Raptor into the snowbank and a tree, but then that's it.

Alex, safe in the cab of the truck, is not crushed, though he has looked death right in the face, and it resembled nothing more than a huge snow blade out of control.

Some of Alex's clothes are caught in the now-closed door of the Raptor, but he's alive. It was indeed "quick," but that's all it was. My nephew is alive. But I know nothing of this; instead, I am drowning on hard ice, my lungs unfulfilled, my breathing dead.

From the cab of the Raptor Alex sees me lying on the ice behind the snowcat. He can't quite work out what has happened. He sees that burgeoning pool of blood coming out of the back of my head. He starts to scream a name.

My name.

Alex has to untangle himself from the clothes that are caught in the truck door that has been slammed shut by the snowcat. He manages to wriggle out of his overalls, leaving him in long johns. With one hand on the snowcat, the other on the Raptor, he throws his body out of the truck and down to the icy ground, and rushes over to where I'm lying.

He looks at me, aghast at the sight. He still can't quite imagine what has happened. But he knows simply by looking that I'm in terrible shape.

Jeremy's fucking dead right now, he thinks.

*   *   *

If this had happened in the presence of someone else, perhaps I wouldn't have survived at all. Luckily for me, Alex seems to slip into a calm, focused frame of mind in a crisis.

When he was on set with me as I filmed the second season of *Mayor of Kingstown*, someone unfortunately had a very serious medical emergency. Alex heard it all on the walkie-talkies people carry around; he was the only PA around at the time and ran to where the man was lying on the ground. Immediately some kind of innate and serene knowledge of what to do kicked in. He made sure the guy was comfortable, made sure he was breathing, told the medics what he knew when they arrived, basically helped save the man's life.

Now, on the ice, he once again somehow stays calm, moving straight into problem-solving mode, remaining focused enough to quickly realize that first he has to ascertain exactly where the damage on my body is.

When he reaches me, he starts to feel along my legs and up and down my back. As he does so, he notices me making grunting sounds, notices slight movement . . .

Alex thinks, *He's not dead*.

But he can also tell that I am critically injured. As his hands travel up my spine, he can feel big spikes jutting through the skin—bump, bump, bump, bump, bump, bump, bump, bump—and realizes that these sharp protrusions signify multiple broken ribs. He touches my neck; he doesn't believe it's broken, though of course it's possible. One leg is broken for sure, pretzeled and mangled.

He doesn't want to move me; it's now maybe thirty seconds, maybe one minute since he reached me.

He thinks, *I don't have my phone. I need to solve this problem right now.* Alex knew that without alerting someone, I would surely die next to him on the driveway.

My nephew could see that I was alive. I had one eye open.

The other eye was on the fucking ground.

*   *   *

I'm not dead. I can feel the gash in the back of my head, and I guess I've broken bones. But I am alive.

In the immediate aftermath, once the machine has passed, I somehow come back into consciousness, and the glimmerings of information start to amass in my brain.

For a start, somehow, I can see my left eye with my right eye; for a flash of a millisecond, I'm confused, then I understand that my left eye has been squeezed out of its orbital socket but has continued operating normally otherwise.

Beyond my eye, as Alex arrives, I, too, begin to mentally take a physical inventory. Seems like maybe just about everything is broken. And the automatic, take-it-for-granted nature of respiration is now a thing of the past, that past being five seconds ago.

I know immediately that this is the most dangerous part of my condition. Without breath, we drown, we die. But try as I might, I simply cannot respirate naturally, let alone normally. Any breath I take will now have to be willed into existence, one inhalation, one groaning exhalation at a time. And with each breath comes that excruciating and disabling pain, as though I've stepped off the edge of a caldera into molten, million-degree rock; I cry out with each breath, primal moans. I suck a little air back in, barely enough to even blow air out, and then with each breath, it feels like I inhale even less air.

Will I panic? It would be the natural thing to do.

THE ONLY OBSTACLE IN YOUR WAY IS YOU. The thought comes to me whole, unfiltered, pure. This is the first of the cheat codes this incident creates for me. *THE ONLY OBSTACLE IN YOUR WAY IS YOU.* It's not as if I thought those words in the form of a cogent sentence—the overwhelming pain short-circuited my grasp of basic language (save some curses)—instead, the mantra *THE ONLY OBSTACLE IN YOUR WAY IS YOU* seemed to float somewhere in my consciousness, informing my next steps, being the framework upon which I could hang all the efforts I knew I'd need to make to survive what had just happened to me.

More cheat codes slip into my scrambling consciousness. Stress is an earthly ego experience, fear-fueled and useless. What I have to use to combat stress is what I call "body awareness"—as an actor I've developed this skill through hard work over many years. It's a crucial part of my job because my body is the instrument by which I do my work. I have a deep understanding of my body and how it operates—and that knowledge, that basic information, gives me something to focus on amid all the pain and disorientation I'm feeling. Knowing my body so intimately gives me a jolt of confidence as lifesaving as any morphine drip. If I had not known myself so well, I know panic would have slipped its icy fingers around my throat, closing it forever. But I understand already, in those first few seconds, that conscious breath will save me. Clearly there is something devastatingly wrong with my respiratory system; I need to get past that immediately. Stress kills more people on this planet than anything; undue stress on the ice that day would have limited my ability to work through the conundrum of how to breathe.

Body mechanics have always been my best friend; I couldn't have known, though, just how crucial my understanding of it would be to any chance I had of living.

And then, like a flood, comes the thought of who I am living *for*. My heart is instantly filled with the images of my family; I don't want to ruin their holiday; I can't disappoint my daughter and the other kids waiting to ski.

A thought comes: *What would happen if I had no one to disappoint, or no one to come back for?*

I know the answer before I even finish thinking it. We are all eternally connected, bound by love and the purest parts of our being, bound by shared history and our innate, unyielding, unchanging energy.

These are like superpowers I discovered in those first few moments after the machine crushed me.

I focus on relaxing my diaphragm; as I start to search across my body to locate which part is responsible for my cramps, my efforts are immediately interrupted by intense stabbing pains. Somehow, I think, *Let me just relax . . . let the spasms calm down so I can get back to breathing.*

(At the time I didn't realize that I had fourteen broken ribs, a punctured lung, a sliced liver, a broken and dislocated collarbone, and a broken shoulder, all of which contributed to my being unable to breathe.)

I hear myself emitting great, guttural groans as I struggle for air. I have to learn, on the fly, to do something that I'd done automatically for more than five decades. It's the only way I'll survive. I already know that.

I start out on that road, hoping it leads me home.

*   *   *

These are the facts of the early morning of New Year's Day, 2023. What I've just described are the first five minutes of the incident, and as I'm learning how to breathe manually, a one-way journey of my survival has just begun. I would be on the ice for the next forty minutes. I wasn't going to die on that ice, most of my family half a mile away, oblivious to this disaster. I was going to live. I was going to overcome any obstacle in my way, whatever it took.

So, I push. I position just right. And with all my might, I groan to exhale, meaning I'm halfway there to my next breath.

3

LAMAZE

I'm the oldest of seven, and there's a significant age gap across all the kids, so I grew up changing diapers, the whole bit: elder brother, caregiver, the good kid.

Something happened in my childhood that took on a strange and almost prophetic meaning post-incident. Because there can't be many teenagers who are made to accompany their mother to Lamaze classes, where pregnant women like my mom are taught how to breathe, how to control pain through explicit, deeply considered breathing.

I was that kid.

Looking back, being taught to breathe to mitigate pain at the age of twelve or thirteen? At the time, I was just annoyed that I got pulled out of soccer practice to head to a local YMCA and hang out with a bunch of expectant mothers. Milestones don't feel like milestones when you're young and mostly dumb.

My mom was pregnant with my sister Nicky, and she didn't think anything of taking me with her—she just really wanted to attend and couldn't leave me at soccer practice while she did so, so she took me.

"Put down your cleats and grab a pillow," she said. "You're coming with."

Being the good boy, I didn't think to argue, so I went, and it ended up being the greatest thing she ever did for me, the most incredible lesson she ever gave me. For a start, at such an early age I got to learn all about the miracle of birth and what women go through. I was lucky to grow up with all women in my household, too, which just lent me all kinds of cheat codes to being a better man. All that extra knowledge and understanding helped make me a more empathetic person, a nurturer; otherwise I'd be way too grizzly. (I'm already grizzly enough as is—I got grizzly down. In fact, I made a career out of it.)

But beyond that, the fact that I learned so early in life the importance of breathing comes back to me now at a very different angle. And to share this extraordinarily intimate moment with my mom at Lamaze class, helping her breathe, helping her to control pain, was an incredibly important and formative experience . . . though it wasn't without its challenges. We were halfway through the lesson, me with a pillow between my mom's legs learning this complicated breathing technique, a gaggle of expectant mothers all splayed out around me on the floor, when out of nowhere a screen came down from the ceiling, and suddenly we're all watching a bathtub birth, the new mother in extremis, all the water exploding from the tub like a whale breaching for air.

I would never unsee this. This was not a YMCA soccer field. This was a different world.

Because I'd never seen anything like this in my life, I redoubled my focus on teaching my mom how to breathe—"he-he, ha-ha, hoo-hoo"—and suddenly the details of counting, inhaling, exhaling, all of it was utterly compelling to this twelve-year-old who didn't really want to watch a woman give birth.

Back then this Lamaze experience wasn't my mom's way of including me into some higher purpose; it was just a practical solution to the logistics of being a single mom (she and Dad had divorced when I was eight, though my dad always lived across the street no matter where we were). But that class ended up being one of the most valuable things she ever did for me as a mother. My mom is amazing and strong, but she's also very stoic and doesn't easily show or share her emotions. And though I can also be quite insular, I am more communicative, more like my dad in that way, so despite the deep love my mom and I have always shared, it wasn't always as easy to get along with her . . . but that Lamaze class is something I've always held with me, a moment of magical connection and intimacy that I cherished. I seemingly had been invited into a secret club: the perspective of my mother in her most intimate moment. Men don't often get such an opportunity; at the time I knew it wasn't normal, but at the same time I knew even then that it was a great honor, though I had no idea how much it would affect my life.

Neither of us could have known that in learning Lamaze together, she effectively saved my life without knowing she was saving it. Because now I was on the ice, and I knew I needed to breathe or I wouldn't make it.

Somehow, so many elements of my life seem to have led straight to those crucial moments.

*　　　*　　　*

I was a latchkey kid, which made me self-sufficient and tenacious. I'd walk home from second grade onward, though I didn't have to be in the house until the streetlights came on, so that gave me a lot of time to roam around Modesto. I was always building a tree house or a go-kart or something (no wonder I'd end up repurposing vehicles all these years later), shooting off a BB gun, getting into scrapes, getting out of them. Being so active, allowing myself to try and fail, made me realize from an early age that *information* was everything, was my savior, would be the thing that saved me from fears, from being too afraid to do things. From as early as seven or eight years old I had a kind of free-flowing energy, a fluidity in my life, especially once I realized that knowledge defeated anxiety every time.

That's not to say I wasn't also a stupid kid. When we weren't throwing rocks at each other, me and my friends played this ridiculous game in which we'd hurl heavy lawn darts or horseshoes in the air and run, praying they didn't land on our heads and kill us. But if I did my homework and I got great grades, I had freedom to do pretty much what I wanted. And even when I got in trouble—I particularly remember breaking a window with a slingshot—I'd reprimand myself (and I told my parents I'd done it, too).

Then there was the day in the fall when I was happily sitting in the front seat (without a seat belt—it was the '70s) while my mom drove. At one point we passed a particularly impressive pumpkin patch, and I pointed it out to my mom, who turned to look, promptly rear-ended the car in front, at which point my head went slam! into the windshield like in those safety videos we all ignored in school.

What I may not have realized then was that all this was just information—you can read about getting a concussion from cracking a windshield all you like, but you know nothing until you actually smack your head hard enough like I did that day. Staying calm, as I did, while my mom freaked out, taught me something about how to react to extremes. No amount of emoting will turn back time to the point where the car doesn't hit the car in front. Once the thing has happened, once the head has cracked the windshield, it's done—from that moment on, it's all about how you react to it, how you react to the information being presented (in my case, in the form of a huge bump and a concussion). Even then, I knew the power of information, and as I went through life, I might fail or I might succeed, but at the very least I was building knowledge. I couldn't have put it that way at age eight or nine, but looking back at my life through the lens of what happened on New Year's Day in 2023, I can see now how the universe left breadcrumbs for me to follow.

I didn't suddenly become someone else right after the incident. We all bring our pasts with us, our ways of dealing with adversity, and that was certainly true of me. So there, on the ice, I brought two crucial things with me to this, the biggest test of my life: the twin gifts of learning how to breathe and not panicking when something goes horribly wrong.

More than anything, I brought my lifelong, crucial savior: *information*. I knew instantly I needed to know what state my body was in.

*   *   *

I had no full sense then what a hot mess my body was in. (The truth was that my collapsed rib cage and my broken and dislocated shoulder and collarbone had worked to compress my lung to the point of suffocation.) Trying to breathe made me realize how bad things were. Yet when I felt an influx of information to the pain center of my brain, rather than making me panic, the jolt of agony made me think, *Figure it out.*

I can't breathe. I can't breathe. I can't breathe.

But I know I have to breathe, so I begin to manipulate my body into certain positions. I think, *Is this just a cramp?*, referring to my extremely painful chest cavity. I can't tell, but I know that pain is limiting my ability to respire. A crucial piece of information grows in my mind like a blooming flower: *If I don't breathe* continually, *and for who knows how long, I'm going to die. So it's imperative I create my own breathing machine, my own life support, and immediately. I must do so, or I'm going to die. If I pass out, I will be dead in a minute, maybe two—with no breathing, my heart will stall, my organs will slow, I'll lose consciousness, and then I'll be unable to manually breathe.*

And I'll be done for.

I start to use every ounce of energy just to push air out so I can suck air back in. I moan with the breath out because it's the only way I know to confirm that I'm actually breathing out—so to add a heaving soundtrack to each exhalation is at least information I can believe in, information that proves that, yes, air came in, and air is now going out.

But each time I suck a little air back in it feels like barely enough to blow air out. As a flash of memory, I bring to mind being kicked in the stomach playing sports in the past, so I do now what I knew to do then: focus on relaxing my diaphragm. As I struggle to breathe, I also try to begin a body inventory again, but I am continually interrupted by agonizing stabbing pains from across my entire body. I'm desperately searching for the body parts responsible for my cramps in case identifying them helps me breathe more easily. I think, *Just relax . . . let the spasms calm . . . get back to breathing . . . relax.*

I have no words other than swears to accompany the guttural groans I use to confirm I'm exhaling. Alex, for his part, having assessed my injuries, and having no phone, knows he must act, and fast.

*   *   *

I hear a voice say, "There's nothing I can do . . . I have to go get help." Alex told me later that there was no way he was going to simply hold my hand until I died. Alex runs.

*   *   *

I am alone.

Panic should arrive. *What is life right now?* It's not what I knew it to be just a few minutes previously. *How do I breathe? How do I think?* Nothing makes sense. *What is this?* I've never felt anything like this in my life.

But somehow the panic never quite arrives.

Alex is gone long enough for me to feel that he's not there.

I am not panicking.

But I am alone. I am lonely.

*   *   *

Alex runs across the street to the closest house. He'd already noticed the garage door was halfway up, but if it had been closed, he was going to run to every single neighbor until he found someone to help. (He didn't know then that the neighbor he chose was just about the only person at home in the entire neighborhood that New Year's morning.)

As Alex approaches, the garage door starts to close, and as he reaches it, in desperation he sort of falls into and under the door.

Imagine the scene from the other side for a moment. The neighbor, Rich Kovach, a pilot home for the holidays, is puttering in his garage. He has been working on his generator, which had been going all weekend, and is now cleaning one of his shotguns. The door is halfway up to help expel the fumes of the generator, but suddenly a stranger in a beanie, shirt, and long johns (his overalls, don't forget, were stuck back in the door of the Raptor) skitters under the closing door.

Rich has no idea who this oddly dressed stranger is, and as he was holding a gun, this could have gone very differently. This is a fairly remote area, and Rich knows there are almost no people about because of the storm. A young man he doesn't recognize bursts into his garage at eight fifty in the morning? And Rich is holding a shotgun?

Fortunately, something about the terror on Alex's face made Rich Kovach point the gun at the ground. Rich had no clue what had happened right outside his house, but he was about to find out.

"What do you want?" Rich says. He has no idea who this person is and why he's just fallen into his garage, though he sure looks like a transient, with his long hair, long johns, and a beanie.

"My uncle . . . I need help," Alex says, out of breath. "He's going to die. He got ran over."

"Calm down, calm down—"

"I *can't* calm down," Alex says. "You need to come over here. We need help."

With that, Rich reopens the garage door, and together with Alex they run as well as they can on the icy road to where I am lying. Rich, instantly understanding the severity of the situation, tells Alex he's going to go find a phone and call 911, and heads back to his house.

I am dimly aware that someone else has arrived, but with Alex back, a flood of love returns.

I am innocent; this is a simple moment.

Please don't leave me.

Please love me.

*   *   *

I focus my energy on continuing to try to breathe the air out and find air to breathe in. Right after the incident I was still in a kind of face down position in the asphalt, which was incredibly painful and further limited my already limited ability to breathe. Instinctually, I motion for Alex to help me move more onto my side, and with a brief trial and error we find a position in which my arm is elevated at a certain angle (this became crucial as the scapula was broken and dislocated). With my arm in that new position, it works to free the lung and mitigate the agony of each breath, meaning I can focus on breathing in, breathing out, breathing in, breathing out, manually breathing, groaning and cursing with each respiration, saving my own life there on the ice.

I keep the panic back behind a dam of pain. I hear the ice underneath me gently melting. It has been maybe ten minutes since I was crushed. I am miles from the nearest hospital, in a remote area at the top of a mountain, a mountain that may well still be closed. The roads are treacherous if they're passable at all. Half a mile away, up the hill, the people I love the most are oblivious to this unfolding disaster.

My name is Jeremy Renner. I am a son, a father, a brother, an uncle, a friend. Everything else matters not at all.

One breath in, one breath out. One breath in, one breath out. One breath in, one breath out.

How long can this go on?

I am about to find out.

*   *   *

Meanwhile, back in Rich's house, his partner, Barb Fletcher, is herself puttering around, watering plants and watching the chickadees at her numerous feeders.

Barb is in a daze that New Year's morning. The previous day she'd been called by her mother to come to a local nursing home, where sadly her mother's brother, Uncle Dick, had just passed away.

When she had arrived at the nursing home, she had found that her uncle's body was still in his room—the undertaker was yet to arrive—and the sight of her uncle devastated her. She'd been very close with him, and this was her first time seeing a dead body, so her mind as she did her chores that next morning was filled with painful images of her mother's brother—in particular, the specific pallor of his skin, an unworldly, un-human color that haunted her every time she closed her eyes.

In her sad reverie, she hardly notices as Rich suddenly appears in the living room.

"Barb!" he says, breathlessly. "You need to get out here right now. Someone's been run over by a snowblower." As Barb stared at him in disbelief, Rich retrieved his phone and proceeded to call 911.

It was 8:55 a.m. when Rich's initial call went through to the emer-gency dispatch in Reno.

RICH: Someone's been run over by a snowcat. Hurry.
DISPATCHER: Okay, tell me exactly what happened.
RICH: So I don't know. Someone's in front of my house on the ground and got run over by a snowcat. He's been crushed. Send paramedics, ambulance.
DISPATCHER: Everyone's on their way right now, okay?

The initial misidentification of "snowblower" had brought to Barb's mind blades and dismembered body parts rather than the crushing hell of a snowcat. In a critical stroke of luck, Barb has worked in the medical field all her life—for a time in a surgical center, and more re-cently with skin cancer patients—and her training instantly kicks in.

She instinctually knows there is going to be blood, so she bolts to the bathroom and grabs a stack of towels, throws her snow boots on, and runs out to the ice-bound driveway. As she runs, she finds herself slipping and falling, and by the time she reaches the scene of the incident, she slips once again and almost lands right next to me.

Seeing the pool of blood, Barb knows how crucial it will be to stop the bleeding as soon as possible. She takes one of her towels and applies it to the gash, cradling my head as she does so. Rich, meanwhile, who "isn't a blood guy," according to Barb, is doing a great job of explaining the situation to the dispatcher on his cell phone. For a moment he also returns to the house to get a pillow and a blanket to try to make me more comfortable.

As Alex holds my arm up, Barb does her best to keep the pressure on the bleeding. It is already an incredible ad hoc team, each doing to the best of their abilities their vital tasks without which who knows what would have happened to me. And each person finds their essential role: Alex helping find the position in which I could breathe, and then on his haunches staying in that position; Barb stemming the bleeding and working to keep me as alert as possible; and Rich relaying to the authorities the seriousness of what is happening and advice for the best way to reach me.

All the while I am focusing on my breathing, gasping and moaning, pushing and struggling, vast waves of pain rushing over me like an unruly ocean.

Pretty quickly Barb realizes the seriousness of the situation. With the roads still mostly snowed out, and with time of the essence, Barb understands that it is critical to my survival that I be helicoptered out—there clearly isn't much time to rely on roads that may or may not be passable, and even if they are, every minute will count.

"Rich," she says, "you need to tell them he needs a CareFlight."

Rich relays this to the dispatcher.

RICH: Listen to me. I need . . . you might want to get life flight out here immediately.

DISPATCHER: Okay, give me one second, okay. Are you with him right now?

RICH: Yes, he's in rough shape.

DISPATCHER: Okay, and how old is he?

RICH: He's probably forty.

DISPATCHER: And is he awake?

RICH: Barely.

DISPATCHER: Okay. Is he breathing?

RICH: He is.

DISPATCHER: Okay.

RICH [to Barb and Alex]: Yes, they're coming.

DISPATCHER: They're coming as fast as they can, okay?

. . .

DISPATCHER: Are there hazards involved?

RICH: I can't hear you. Say again?

DISPATCHER: Are there chemicals or other hazards involved?

RICH: No. No, no, no, no, no, no. Just a lot of blood.

DISPATCHER: Is anyone pinned?

RICH: No.

DISPATCHER: Okay.

RICH: We just need someone here right away with lifesaving techniques.

DISPATCHER: We have help coming from all over right now.

RICH: All right.

DISPATCHER: Does he appear to be completely awake?

RICH: Yes.

DISPATCHER: And then are there any obvious injuries?

RICH: Yeah. Oh my God, yes.

DISPATCHER [hearing Rich's frustration]: I just have to ask the questions. They're on their way. And is there any serious bleeding?

RICH: Yes.

The uniqueness, the unfathomability of what had happened to me, can be heard in the advice the dispatcher then gave to Rich—she seemed to be under the impression that there had been some kind of car accident.

DISPATCHER: Okay. Paramedics have been on the way this whole time . . . I'm going to tell you exactly what to do next. I do need to advise, do not splint any injuries and then do not move him unless he's in danger. And then for everyone's safety, stand clear of approaching traffic and if it's safe to do so, turn on flashing hazards.

The repetitive nature of the dispatcher's questions, though sometimes frustrating to those in the traumatic situation, nevertheless serve to give the approaching paramedics the clearest picture possible from their distance.

DISPATCHER: Where is he bleeding from?
RICH: I don't know. I can't tell. His head. [to Barb and Alex] Oh, whoa, whoa. Easy, easy, easy, easy. It's on the inside. Okay.
DISPATCHER: I'm going to tell you how to stop the bleeding and listen carefully to make sure we do it right. Get a clean, dried-off towel and then tell me when you have it.
RICH: We've got it. We've got it wrapped here.
DISPATCHER: Put it right on the wound and press down firmly and then don't lift it up to look.
RICH: It's a head wound . . . [to Barb] Just press firmly, Barb.
DISPATCHER: What other injuries does it look like he has?
RICH: I don't know.

Rich turned to Alex to try to get more information.

RICH [to Alex]: Tell me what happened.

It's incredible to hear Alex in the background of the 911 call. Though I can tell he's freaked out, he's also able to calmly describe as much as he knows.

ALEX [to Rich]: He got completely crushed by it, under the cat.

Rich, in turn, does an incredible job relaying this information to the dispatcher.

RICH [to the dispatcher]: Okay, so he got caught under . . . we're talking about one of these huge cats used on the snow mountain, so he got crushed underneath of it . . . Yeah, there's a lot of blood over here, so you've got to get somebody over here immediately.
DISPATCHER: We have lots of people coming . . .
RICH: . . . And tell them to be careful. We're in the middle of the road so when they come down from the top, it's on quite an incline. They don't want to run over us while we're in the road.
DISPATCHER: Okay.
RICH: It's very icy. Tell them to be careful.
. . .
RICH: He said he's got rib issues. His right side, I see it. He got crushed up on his right side. His ribs are broken.
DISPATCHER: His right chest?
RICH: Yeah, his right chest and the upper torso. His ribs look like they might be crushed. He's got a head wound as well.

Later, Barb would admit that with the image of her uncle in her mind, she just couldn't face going through that kind of loss again the very next day. It was imperative to her that she save this stranger's life. She told me that her "mom instinct" kicked in (her son is a serviceman), so she keeps talking to me. She is rubbing my forehead, too—apparently at some point I looked up at her as if to try to recognize who is performing this act of pure love for me.

Alex remains in deep shock, but on his haunches, he keeps my arm at that saving angle, helping me to breathe. Barb is talking, rubbing my arm anytime my eyes grow heavy.

"Stay with me," she says. "They're going to be here. Stay with me. They're coming. Help's coming."

And Rich remains in constant contact with dispatch.

DISPATCHER: I am going to stay on the line with you as long as I can. Watch him very closely [in case] he changes. If he becomes less awake or starts getting worse, tell me immediately and tell me when the paramedics are right there with him . . . Keep pressure on the wounds.

RICH: How much farther are they?

DISPATCHER: We have the Truckee Meadows truck coming, but we also have Incline coming as well.

Rich, realizing that both Truckee Meadows and Incline Village are a full fifteen miles from where we are (though in opposite directions from each other), finds his frustration with the situation building, fueled as it is by the trauma and my deteriorating condition.

RICH: Truckee Meadows? I could have taken him in my truck to the hospital, Jesus.

The dispatcher lets Rich gripe and continues to try to keep everyone calm.

DISPATCHER: We have our closest units already responding . . . and we also have CareFlight as well coming.

RICH: Tell them they can land at the Tanenbaum Event Center . . . There's enough room over there that CareFlight can land there.

Still in the background I continue to try to breathe, moaning through each exhalation. Rich is increasingly frantic.

RICH: He's got broken ribs. He's probably got a punctured lung . . .

Wondering what else he can do, Rich heads back to the house; while there, the dispatcher continues to ask questions.

DISPATCHER: How many people are out with them right now?

RICH: Two people and the victim. There's three total.

DISPATCHER: Is he lying in the snow?

RICH: Yes, he's lying in the middle of the street.

DISPATCHER: You're in the house. Can you grab him a blanket or something to at least try and help keep him a little bit warm? We don't want to move him.

RICH: He's got all snow equipment on, we've got towels, a pillow. He's in rough shape. I mean he's in a rough shape . . .

DISPATCHER: I'm keeping everyone updated with everything you're telling me as well. And I told them the Tanenbaum Event Center would be ideal for landing. I let CareFlight know that as well.

RICH: But ma'am, please tell me somebody's coming up from down in Reno, not from Truckee, oh my God.

DISPATCHER: Yes, they are.

Rich heads back out to the driveway.

RICH [to me]: Hang in there, brother. The pain's one thing as long as you keep breathing, man. Keep fighting.

With my arm securely in position, my focused breathing becomes slightly less excruciating, but only marginally. Each breath is the equivalent of the effort it takes to complete a full push-up, and little did I know that I'd embarked on almost forty-five minutes of this intense, agonizing labor. Nevertheless, my new way to breathe is now set. As I struggle to maintain consciousness, in the far distance I can hear a woman's voice; as she talks, she keeps pressure on the back of my head. Her voice is quietly panicked. A man is talking on a cell phone. My nephew holds my arm.

I can't adequately describe the effort it takes to make one breath. On the 911 call you get a small sense of it—me moaning as if in agony in the background, though in fact the truth is that each groan is my confirmation that I'm exhaling—but words might fail me to further describe how it feels to manually inflate your chest cavity every few seconds for forty-five minutes. Then there's the fact that every breath I struggle through is of frozen, oxygen-depleted air. It's harder to breathe at 7,300 feet than at sea level at the best of times—above 8,000 feet everyone is susceptible to high-altitude sickness because of the scarcity of oxygen, but newcomers to Camp Renner often remark on their shortness of breath until they acclimatize. I am also in blind pain with multiple broken bones, I sport a major gash in the back of my head, and have one eye hanging out . . .

But something in my life force drives me on. I don't mean to claim it was superhuman—it was brutal and bloody and ugly and grinding and excruciating and devastating, a battlefield on which my body lay pulverized, my soul the soul of a soldier who wonders if this, right here, would be the place of his last moments, coming up against the end of breath, the end of consciousness, the end of struggle, the culmination of a life on an ice field, surrounded by my dear nephew and two strangers, but a death unknown to my daughter, my parents, my siblings, my dearest friends. Would this really be how it ended? A crackpot slip trying to jump into the moving cab of a massive machine, all the roads I'd been on—latchkey childhood, loner adolescence, fear-fighting early adulthood, LA struggle, breaking through, the rise of fame, the homes, the loves, the work, the machines, the music—all paths now converging on a barren, ice-bound driveway, on a day I'd hoped to help my family escape into a New Year of ski slopes and hot chocolate?

Was this really it? Would this ignominious incident be my final act?

Alex holds my arm.

In my agony, I still maintain a kind of blind hope. Despite what had just happened, and with each breath in thrall to the fear that this is where the story ends, I still find in myself a level of what I can only describe as optimism. Though my body is completely smashed, my eye hanging out, every breath an agonizing push-up from the depths of drowning, still my mind manages to delve into a kind of instinctual problem-solving. First up had been the breathing, and once I got that regulated, I was able to think about the damage to my eye—and what I thought was, "I'll worry about that later."

One of my legs is twisted all around a few times this way and that, and I know that doesn't look good. The other leg looks like it should hurt, and it doesn't, which is even more worrying. (I thought, *Yeah, that's going to hurt later, too.*)

But hope keeps intruding. I think, *All right, maybe this cramp will go away, and I'll walk back up to the house and apologize and tell everyone that we're probably not going to be able to go skiing today after all.* A few minutes after that thought comes another related one: *Maybe the cramp's not going away and maybe somebody's going to have to help me back to the house?* Then more thoughts: *I'm going to need an Epsom salt bath and get some ice on this eyeball.*

It may seem hard to believe, but I genuinely thought that if I could just rid myself of "the cramp," I could probably rest up for a day or two and be in good shape to continue the vacation.

I remain in my breathing rhythm, but darker thoughts sometimes intrude through each painful inhalation: *I don't think I'm going to make it down the driveway and tell the family,* or worse, *Am I going to live like I'm in some kind of petri dish, a fucking science experiment? Will I just be a brain inside a ruined body? A vegetable?* I don't live in those dark places too long; each time the darkness intrudes, I go back to focusing on my breathing, and doing and redoing my body inventory, trying to figure out exactly where the damage is and how bad it might be.

Part of my job as an actor and athlete is to focus on the body. It's the one "tool" we bring to our job—everything we do on set is contingent on our physical presence, on controlling and understanding our corporeal form. So already knowing my body as part of my professional life served me well that morning on the ice. But what do I do now? My thinking—a kind of tenacity tempered by lots of realism—existed prior to the incident. My push always has been for more data, more information—I've never exactly been Captain Optimism about anything. I just think you set yourself up to fail with too much confidence. I'm not the one who joshes people along with a peppy, "Come on, guys!" Actually, I want to shoot that kind of person, the one who's perky and positive every single morning and all day long. I know those super-positive people, and I'm not much of a fan of someone who is constantly looking on the bright side.

Instead, I'm a realist, the guy who in bad moments bites down and grits through.

But I can still find hope in an honest assessment of raw reality, and that was what was happening even on the ice. And I try to make the best out of something by taking action rather than wishing it was better, like an overly optimistic person might do. To make things better, to achieve the things you want to achieve, to push through and past obstacles, you have to *do* something. You cannot be inactive. You will die. Complacency is death; it is the opposite of life; it is what keeps us stuck in situations that make us unhappy.

These are not the thoughts of a Marvel hero, or a Superman. They're just mine, the DNA of a man who believes in cautious optimism, looking always for what's actionable.

So yes, as I lay there, crushed, smashed, at the edge of death, I still kept thinking, *If I can just release this cramp, and get some ice on my eye, I think I'll be able to walk back to the house.*

* * *

Meanwhile, up at Camp Renner, folks are waking up, getting coffee, preparing for the day, the year. Alex and I are the only ones missing—as far as anyone knows, we're still out there opening the road, making an escape route, an uncle and his nephew clearing drifts, paving paths, moving mountains of snow, back and forth, getting snowmobiles out of snowbanks, cars deiced and ready to roll. No one thinks anything of anything; there's breakfast to make, kids to get ready, recaps of the snowball fight the previous night to be shared, how strange it was to watch the ball drop at 12:03 but really 3:03 in Times Square, the fact that finally the air has cleared, the snow has stopped, and the slopes await.

The reality for me is different. Every breath is dragged from me as if I must carve it out of stone. A stranger holds a towel to my head; my nephew squats, keeping my arm in position. A man is saying, "He's going to need CareFlight. Urgently. Please get here."

Each second, each minute—one, two, five, ten, twenty—drags like molasses, but despite the unbearable slowness of time, at least time is passing.

I face my fears one breath at a time. But then, I'd trained myself for years to look fear in the face and overcome it. I don't know what that morning would have been like if I hadn't already made a commitment to face each fear and work to disable it.

But what-ifs get me nowhere. All that matters is my next breath.

4

SWIMMING WITH SHARKS

As I lay on the ice that New Year's morning, my long road to recovery had already begun. In agony, and gasping for every breath, it wasn't as if that was clear to me immediately, but in retrospect that's when it began. The second the machine cleared me and left me alone on the driveway, I was bound upon a one-way path.

In looking back on the incident, I have wanted to make sense of who that person was who had just suffered such a catastrophic set of injuries. None of us show up to our life's experiences as newborns. We each bring with us a set of coordinates from a life lived. These coordinates might not be easily recognized in the moment, but in telling this story I have come to plot a map of my life to see who I was before the incident and who I became after it.

I've learned I was lucky that many facets of my character that were already in place helped me survive that day. Life had readied me to find a way to push through the agony and terror so that I could reach safety, so that I could breathe my way to being rescued and, after that, bulldoze my way through my recovery, hitting milestone after milestone so that my own recovery could spur the recovery of those around me.

Because the deepest truth of what happened that morning is that it didn't just happen to me. First it happened to Alex, who had had to face his own demise ("please be quick, please be quick"), then find his uncle apparently dead on the driveway, then rush for help, then hold his arm in a certain position for nearly an hour. All that trauma—all those things no one should ever have to see—and still he had to make crucial, lifesaving decisions.

Then, what happened to me also happened to Barb and Rich. They had been waking up into a new year, innocently going through their morning, though with heartaches of their own. Barb especially, who wasn't even twenty-four hours past having to see her beloved uncle laid out on a nursing home bed, his life over.

Less immediately, but no less powerfully, were the rest of my family and friends. My daughter, Ava, innocently waking into a clear-sky day, wondering where her dad was; my mom, away celebrating the birth of a grandchild, not yet aware that her firstborn was chasing death two hundred miles to the east. My dad, who would be the first, along with Kym, to the hospital. My other siblings and their kids, who would have to face the trauma of my accident in their own ways; Dave Kelsey, Rory Millikin, my friends across the world . . . What happened to me didn't happen to me in a vacuum. In missing that jump, in falling to the earth, in being pulverized by a 14,000-pound machine, in facing death on the ice, and in the coming months of recovery, I had invited the people I loved into a hellscape of my own making.

And the only way I could save each of those people from that hell was to survive in the first instance, and then power through recovery, dragging them with me as I did so. So no, I have never considered this incident mine alone; it was something visited upon the innocent people around me, and in order to help them heal, I had to bring every ounce of my strength to bear, every second of every day. For me there was never an option of relaxing, of not fighting harder than I've ever fought for anything.

Yes, it was an "accident"—though I think of it as an *incident*, because I think things happen for a reason—but whatever I call it, I'm still aware I caused it. It wasn't on purpose, and I don't think it was reckless, but I have to live with not applying the hand brake on the snowcat, I have to face up to the fact that "Not today, motherfucker" turned into all this. I know what I did to Alex; I'm deeply conscious of what I did to my family. I know I fucked up a New Year's promise to the kids; I know the trauma I put upon people. I love them so much, care about them so much, and I know I did something so bad to them—they, in turn, feel terrible because of something that happened to me. I was trying to save Alex, but still I created a disaster for them, and I broke their hearts.

I put images in their minds. I made everyone face the fragility of life when all we're trying to do is to get through a day.

From the very beginning, then, it was my job to work to erase those images as quickly as I could. My job as an actor has always been about immersing myself into somebody else's perspective. I had no choice after the incident to see what I'd wrought on the Renner family and the wider set of people I cared about. And witnessing the pain I'd caused, I had only one choice (and it wasn't really a choice; it was just how it had to be): I had to change the narrative, rewrite the script, reshoot the ending. The only way to move past it would be to move past it together. Everyone close to me was injured as much as I was in different ways, and we would all have to do a whole bunch of healing. We all spend so much of our lives trying not to feel something, trying not to feel anything, just to get through; that couldn't happen here. We had to feel together, and recover together.

Could that Jeremy Renner, the one innocently clearing snow on the first day of the year, draw upon everything that had come together to make him who he was and somehow heal the people he loved the most?

*　　*　　*

If you just give me one job to do, I'm going to do my darndest to be excellent at it, and I say this without arrogance: I'm going to win. Throughout my life, the things that I've been interested in, I excelled at quickly, and that's what kept me interested: a self-fulfilling prophecy. This has tended to make it seem as though I'm good at a lot of things, but that's not actually true. I just don't do things I suck at. To my mind, that's what hobbies are: something you do that you probably suck at because you can't commit to it being a central part of your life. I think a hobby is the worst thing someone could do—at least that's certainly true for me. I only want to do things that most command my time and attention.

I grew up in a bowling center, McHenry Bowl, on McHenry Avenue in Modesto, at the northern edge of California's Central Valley. My dad ran McHenry Bowl for years, and my whole family worked there at some point in their life. Dad was an okay bowler but great at teaching it, and my mom was a good bowler, too—she has always been an athlete.

Growing up in that environment made me a decent bowler. Even though I was underdeveloped as a boy—I didn't hit puberty until I was sixteen—by twelve years old I could rip a sixteen-pound ball pretty well, and my technique was solid. Being a lefty, I knew that there's more oil on the left-hand side of the lane, so I'd need to bowl the ball a little straighter and not curve it so much (because the oil adds spin). I learned how different lanes behaved, where to land my foot to maximize the efficiency of the delivery . . . all to the point where I became good enough by that young age to bowl against professionals in a competitive league.

But too often I found myself being dissatisfied with my performance—if I didn't get my average, I would kick the ball return, curse, and generally have a meltdown. If I shot two 260s (300 is the best you can do), and then a 185, all I'd think about was that 185 . . . there were times I was my own worst enemy. Self-doubt turned into hatred, hatred into anger, anger into rage, and, being twelve, I just wasn't emotionally mature enough to handle these feelings. I'd think, *Screw this sport—either I need to learn to bowl much better or I'm going to do something else.* My dad could see that I wasn't having any fun, so some days he would take me to a less-used lane at the far end of McHenry and show me how the oil affected my bowling, or he would try to help me see that what mattered were the two 260s I could shoot on an oily lane, not the 185. But still, I couldn't get past the feeling that I should be hitting twelve strikes in a row every time for the elusive maximum 300 score. In the end, I walked away from bowling, and to this day I still have a complicated relationship with the sport—I feel fine ripping some pockmarked eight-pound balls down a lane with my daughter, and if somebody really wants to learn how to bowl I can teach them, but my relationship with bowling is not the same as other people's relationship with bowling. These days if I bowl a 110, I'm fine with it, but even then, I can still remember that heavy feeling when I'd hit thirty pins under my average.

To this day I think finding out what you *don't* want to do is just as important—maybe more important—than finding what you're good at. I think we all know people who don't have a strong idea of what they want to do or are really struggling to find out. I managed to work out early that I didn't want to bowl anymore because I couldn't do it to the level I knew I was capable of. That's also why I can't just look on bowling as a "hobby" and enjoy it the way recreational bowlers can—I've seen the highest standards, and was on my way to reaching them, but it happened too early, and I didn't have the maturity to let it come to me in an organic way. The upshot was that bowling became frustrating rather than joyful, so I walked away from it. "I just don't do things I suck at." (That I was actually really good at it doesn't mean I didn't suck at being the *best* at it.)

Though this might signal a kind of "giving up" mentality, what it actually meant for me was that I was able to develop a confidence in the things I could actually excel at. This confidence came from two things: information, and always having that safe landing spot of love with my family. From an early age I've always known that my family will always be there for me no matter what happens in my life, that they will always literally and metaphorically take me to a less-used lane and show me that I matter, never mind what wrong choices I might make—whatever it is, they're still there to always love me. I think of my family as the mattress on the ground saving me from hitting the earth. My parents, especially, gave me—gave all of us Renners—a safe landing spot of love, no matter what.

My parents were very different from each other. My dad is a student of religions, an intellectual butterfly, the kind of guy who wants to talk about feelings, and is happiest wandering along a path to look at the trees and nature and discuss what he finds. Energetically he's very Baloo the Bear–like (but Baloo in the movie, not the sourpuss from Kipling's book).

He's a wanderer, but he is also a teacher.

One day at McHenry his sister, my aunt Nancy, caught me smoking—I was probably ten years old. I knew I was in trouble when I heard my name being called over the bowling alley speaker: "Jeremy Renner to the front desk."

When I showed up, my dad said, "Son, you want to smoke? Fine— here are your choices: You can either smoke this entire cigar, or you can eat this . . ." and he handed me a big old stogey and one of Aunt Nancy's cigarettes.

Negotiations ensued—there was no way I was smoking an entire cigar as I could barely light a cigarette—and I ended up eating a tiny bit of the rolling paper that my dad had scrunched up into a little ball. It was nasty, but his point was made, and it was made with love. Once I'd somehow swallowed it, he bought me an iced Cherry Coke and gave me a huge hug. It was a simple little lesson, but I've taken it with me through life, because knowing you always have love, no matter how much you screw up, is a huge thing for a kid (and the adult he'd grow up to be).

Later, he'd give me an even bigger gift.

By the time I was ready to think about college, my dad had given up the bowling alley and had gone back into education, working at Cal State University Stanislaus in Turlock, California. No one in my family could afford higher education and I didn't want to go into huge student debt not knowing what I wanted to study, so Dad encouraged me to enroll at MJC, my local junior college, and find out where my passions lay.

And there he gave me the greatest gift my father ever gave me. He urged me to fail. His advice was, you must take at least twelve units—

units that would enable me transfer to a four-year school—but, beyond those, try anything and everything and go FAIL! So I followed his advice and tried a bunch of courses—twenty-six units, actually—and that is how I discovered acting.

I ended up taking a double major: psychology and theater. I starred in *Orphans, Sister Gloria's Pentecostal Baby*, and *The Wizard of Oz*, and my life's trajectory was set. But that would never have happened without my father's admonition to "just go try stuff; go fail, son." The confidence that gave me is impossible to quantify—backed up as it was by love, knowing that I had the freedom to find my way on my own.

*   *   *

I was supercompetitive as a kid. It didn't matter that I was the older brother to Kym, I was always determined to beat her in any game we played; but it didn't end there. As kids we had stickers with our names on them, and I'd cover Kym's stuff with my stickers, or else I'd sneak into our junk drawer and sell her whatever I found—I remember selling her a broken watch once. When my friends came around, they'd make fun of Kym—I would join in, of course—and I fear I really tortured her, yet she adored me, and I secretly adored her. But one day we got into a fight, and I slapped her—she, in turn, threw a pair of scissors at me. Kym called Mom at work, who got on the phone with me.

"You're grounded," Mom said. "Go to your room and stay there."

And because I obeyed my mom no matter what, off I went.

Unfortunately—or fortunately, for this introvert—Mom forgot she'd sent me to my room. During dinner, my sister said, "Mom, you do know Jeremy's still in his room, right?"

This wasn't a one-off, either—Mom was the practical one and used to ground me all the time and then forget. But underpinning it all was a real and practical love—one side, my father, with his head sometimes in the clouds, and on the other, my mom, running the house, doling out discipline, making sure we became the best people we could be.

So to have that kind of love always available filled me as a child with
confidence . . . and then as an adult, the pragmatic part of confidence
kicked in, which for me came from information. Information is what
squelches fear. We are only afraid of the unknown. Ignorance, or lack
of experience, is simply a lack of data. Not all information takes away
fear, but any amount of it can dampen the insecurities and the killing
unknowns of fear.

I was so lucky in college to study psychology and theater. Both dis-
ciplines became my tools to use as I moved forward in life. Each gave
me a greater understanding of my own footprint on this planet, my own
identity, my own strengths, my own weaknesses, my belief systems. I'd
studied all religions growing up because of my dad and ended up appre-
ciating all of them, though no single faith was for me—but at least I got
information about how to live from them.

But still, as a young man I was sometimes held back by fear, as so
many of us are when we set out on our journey through life. I wasn't
going to let fear rule me, though. I think this can be true of a lot of
introverts—at times I'd have to ask myself, "What's stopping me from
doing what I want in my life?" I was seeking energy, as many twenty-
year-olds might; I wanted to find my own worth, but I realized that I
was carrying around a whole box of fears, and I could see so clearly the
damage those fears could do—they were holding me back from living
the life I wanted to. I'd always been a quieter kid than most, interior,
an observer—I found myself paying a lot of attention to the world, deep
thinking, and part of that thinking was being aware that I was bound by
certain fears—whether fear of success, intimacy, loss, sharks, snakes, or
heights. It could be anything, really.

By the time I was twenty-one, I was done being trammeled by that
emotion. I needed to make each fear tangible so I could own it instead
of it owning me. So I made a conscious decision to codify my fears and
face them one by one. I would write down each fear, and then work to
face it as best I could until I could check it off as no longer a fear, or less
powerful at least.

It wasn't an easy process. Once I'd identified the fear, I had to take steps every day to combat it and check it off the list. I ended up spending a decade, every day, focusing on my fears and confronting them. I'm not going to lie: Every day it sucked. It was a chore, and it was not something I ever *wanted* to do. Nobody ever wants to attack their fears. But I did want to be free of them. So I forced myself to do it every day. Whenever something would pop up, even the smallest of things, I'd face it.

And after nearly a decade of doing it, I realized that fear is driven almost entirely by the unknown. Survival is everything for humans, so it's natural to have that visceral fear reaction to danger, to the unknown, but I wanted to harness that reaction by understanding what I was afraid of so that I could live my life more fully and with more confidence. Fear can control our lives, and I didn't want fear to control my life, so I just kicked its ass; I owned it. When I found myself getting afraid of something, I decided to simply go right at it, right into it, until it was no longer scary.

It became a very practical, visceral effort. For example, I knew I could sing, but I was afraid of singing in front of people, so to combat it, I'd sing karaoke five, six days a week. They'd call my name, and my hands would be sweating, but I'd stride up to the little stage, take the microphone, and belt. I wasn't the only one who was terrified. I would sing karaoke with friends who'd been Broadway singers, but karaoke is a different animal, because none of us performers were in character—we had to sing as ourselves. (By the way, my attempts at karaoke were so successful that I almost became a member of boy band O-Town—I auditioned over the phone [and straight out of the shower, I might add—thank God it was the years before Zoom calls], but I still held on to the dream of being a successful actor, so I didn't follow up.)

I can't even recall all the things I wrote down. I know one that was a whole process to face was the age-old fear of sharks that so many of us have. Me? I went and got a scuba diving license, then a master diver's license, and then I swam with sharks—and yes, sure enough, I watched as a shark ate a damn seal, right in front of me. I was off the coast of

California at the time, near Catalina Island, and it was terrifying, but I stayed in the scene, horrified but fighting my fear.

*   *   *

That karaoke bar also had a mechanical bull, and I'd ride it because if you stayed on long enough, you'd win a couple hundred bucks, which I needed.

Another fear overcome.

When you lived on donut holes, like I did back then, two hundred dollars was a lot of dough. At one point in my early years in Los Angeles (I moved there right after college to try to make it as an actor), I only had five dollars a month for food, but I knew that you could get fourteen donut holes for a buck, so I'd live on one a day. I also knew you could get two cheeseburgers at McDonald's for twenty-five cents on Tuesdays, and a huge bag of almonds for next to nothing from Ralph's. I lived for a while without electricity or running water, too, let alone *hot* water. This was 1995-ish, and I'd be counting pennies, splitting bills with my roommate. I would get on the phone with my mom, and she'd start rambling on about nothing—the dog has an infected ear, Kyle's going to soccer practice, Nicky's at softball practice—and I'd just be thinking about money.

Eventually I'd stop her and say, "Mom, honestly, *why* are you calling me?"

There would be a long, pregnant pause.

"I just want to tell you that I love you," she said, and I instantly felt like an asshole.

"Well," I said, filled with guilt for cutting her off, "can you tell me that first and then I'm happy to hear about the dog's infections . . . ?"

Some boxes of fear you can't check off altogether—fear of loss, fear of success, fear of heartbreak are just some that come to mind.

Another fear was being told no (fear of rejection)—as a struggling actor I was told no all the time. But at least I was pursuing what I loved, which was acting—I didn't have to earn a living as a bookkeeper at Foster Farm Dairy doing accounts payable and receivable like my mom had to. I knew that wasn't her dream, but she struggled for money, too, so she took action (I know where I got it from). She'd still try to send me a hundred bucks here or there, which was a lot for her back then.

Even though I was barely paying my bills, I was getting enough jobs to build my career, and I was doing something I loved. And I was checking off those fears one by one. What I think I developed in that decade-long process was a kind of fortitude, a belief, a focus, a clarity in what I wanted to do and who I wanted to be. I had always been a freethinking boy, a free-range child, the latchkey kid. For as long as I could remember, I had been the captain of my own ship, still a little shy, still sometimes a loner.

The backup I had was that I always landed on a bed of love with my family. That's what gave me the confidence to move to LA in the first place, to fight my fears, to stick it out even when it meant eating donut holes and bags and bags of almonds.

My early career was filled with work, but on the small side. I was in a couple of things on UPN and Fox, and then a made-for-TV film called *A Friend's Betrayal*. I did one-off slots in a show called *Angel* and *Time of Your Life*, which was a teen drama, *Party of Five* spin-off that lasted about five months. When I got the lead in *Dahmer* in 2002, I was paid $50 a day to make that movie—we shot it in thirteen days on a budget of $250,000. But it was the love of the work that kept me at it, and Kathryn Bigelow saw me play Jeffrey Dahmer and would eventually cast me in *The Hurt Locker* because she'd liked what she saw.

And those fears? The process by which I faced each of those fears—writing them down and checking them off on a piece of paper—eventually became imprinted on my inner life, became a *way* of life.

Everything I was learning about facing fears came down to *energy*. I realized quickly that it takes immense energy to face a fear. To jump out of a plane with a parachute on takes more than just jumping. You have to gas up your car, drive out to the landing spot, get in the plane, soar to 10,000 feet, attach yourself to a stranger, trust that stranger, and then jump out—you can't just be up in a plane and jump. Energy, yes, and confidence, but that list on that piece of paper, the one with the growing list of check marks, became my way of conspiring with the universe. Fear was no longer just a feeling swimming around in my head—it was something I'd been able to wring out of my soul. And eventually I stopped checking things off because facing my fears had found a solid place in my body and my consciousness. You do something every day for a decade it becomes who you are. I was now able to go right into the eye of pretty much any storm and not allow fear to dictate my life. I had completely changed my relationship to fear to the point where I no longer even thought about it. It was no longer a piece of paper; it was inside me, a pattern in my body to write into it.

With that new pattern in my body came a crucial clarity of intention. When you really know what you're focused on, you can manifest what you truly want in your life. The trick is to get out of our own damn way. I guarantee that we are the biggest obstacle to achieving the things we want to achieve. But because we're often not clear in what we want, if we're off course or unfocused, we're just going to be like an electron bouncing around the nucleus of a cell, or a planet floating around this star of fire, forever burning energy as we just flail around through life.

This is not good.

"Clarity of intention" is a phrase that's now deeply ingrained in my brain. (Amazingly, "don't forget to breathe" was another one that was etched in me when I was young.) These phrases are a part of my DNA because they're the root of every action I perform.

I could have felt crushed by what happened to me on the ice (excuse the pun). My soul might have been crushed by it as much as my body was. I may have thought, *This is the big disaster. I'm going to give up.* But I had that fight in me, that fire. It came from all those years of facing fears, of Ava and my parents and my siblings, that great mattress of love on the ground, saving me from hitting the earth. It couldn't save me from the snowcat, but from the moment that terrible machine rolled away from me, my clarity of intention was to breathe—just that, to breathe, to work out how to get from one second to the next.

Yes, my body was a wreck on the icy asphalt of a disastrous New Year's. But a lifetime of facing fears was about to pay off.

* * *

This was the biggest thing I'd ever written on that fear list: Could I breathe long enough to make it? Could I survive long enough for paramedics to get to me on this snowbound morning? Could I recover well enough to not be living like a science experiment? Would I walk, run, think clearly?

Would I see Ava again? Would I see my mother again? My father? My siblings, Dave, Rory?

Could I make it to the next breath so that someone could come and help me?

As I faced those fears with each exhalation, Rich continued to talk to emergency dispatch. In the background of the recording, you can hear me "groaning," though in reality it was me making sure I breathed in and out, in and out.

RICH: You still there?

DISPATCHER: I'm still here . . . They're coming up Mount Rose right now, sir.

RICH [to Barb and Alex]: They're coming up Mount Rose right now.

BARB [to me]: You'll be fine.

RICH [as I swear in pain]: "Oh, fuck" is about right.

RICH [to the dispatcher]: Can you give me an ETA?

DISPATCHER: It's hard to give an ETA just because of the snow on the mountain. I don't know how quick they're able to go.

RICH: His breaths are getting shorter, so please.

. . .

DISPATCHER: Has the bleeding been controlled on his head yet?

RICH: We haven't opened it up to look.

DISPATCHER: Okay. Good job. You guys are doing great.

. . .

RICH: How much longer, ma'am?

DISPATCHER: They're just about to come up . . . They're about half a mile from that hairpin turn that we were talking about.

RICH [to me]: You are going to be all right, brother. This is just pain. Just deal with that. You'll be all right. We'll get you out of here. All right. It's not how we wanted to meet you though . . .

BARB [to me]: Are you warm enough? You're cold. Are you cold?

RICH: They're almost here.

DISPATCHER: And is he still awake?

RICH: Yeah . . . [to Barb and Alex]: They should be here in a minute.

DISPATCHER: How's he doing?

RICH: Shallow breaths. A lot of pain. He's conscious. Okay, we've got him covered in blankets. His head's covered. He's been drifting off.

DISPATCHER: Is he starting to kind of drift off into sleep?

RICH: Yeah. [to me]: Stay awake.

I still had to face the ultimate fear of all. As my temperature dropped, as the EMTs struggled to make it up the mountain, as each breath became harder, as each broken bone screamed out with growing agony, I found I could still fall farther.

As I lay on the ice, my heart rate slowed, and right there, on that New Year's Day, unknown to my daughter, my sisters, my friends, my father, my mother, I just got tired. After about thirty minutes on the ice, of breathing manually for so long, an effort akin to doing ten or twenty push-ups per minute for half an hour . . . that's when I died.

I died, right there on the driveway to my house.

5

TAILLIGHTS

Though I'd broken more than thirty bones and lost six quarts of blood (I'd find out the true extent of the injuries only later), an even greater danger to me as the minutes dragged by on the ice was hypothermia—in fact I was probably closer to dying from hypothermia than anything else. With the temperatures that morning hovering around freezing, and my body in shock, stuck on an icy driveway, the killing cold began to dangerously bite.

Barb continues to keep her eyes set on me, holding my head and talking to me.

"Just keep breathing," she says, "just breathe. Just take shallow breaths. Take shallow breaths. Stay with us. Keep your eyes open," repeating these phrases like a mantra, rubbing my hand, rubbing my forehead, just to keep me alert. But then she notices the color of my skin significantly change—she described it as a gray-green color, and I close my eyes for a few seconds.

It was the same color skin she'd seen on her uncle the previous day—the exact same. *This just happened the day before*, she thought, her heart sinking, a sob in her throat. She was desperately trying to wake me up, but to this day she insists that, in her words, "I lost you—in my heart, I felt like you were gone."

In an interview with Diane Sawyer later Barb said, "He just kept closing his eyes. At one point I was holding his head—I wouldn't take my eyes off of him because I didn't want him to drift off . . . Then he got a clammy feel to him and turned this gray-green color. I feel in my heart I lost him for a second. He closed his eyes. I really feel he did pass away for a couple of seconds."

When Alex had first reached me, he'd thought I was dead, but for him, the initial fear had quickly morphed into a calmer sense of "we're going to push through this." But for those moments where I stopped breathing, where my color changed—Alex described it later as "green to purple," a terrible moment—he found himself leaning in even more closely so he could perhaps hear my last words. So far, the only last words I'd uttered had been the ones I'd been using to help expel the air from my broken lungs: "Hookers, whores, and hamburgers," among other colorful expletives. (It was the huffing effort of the "H" sound that was working for me, just so you know.)

I make no apologies.

*　　*　　*

I know I died—in fact, I'm sure of it. (When the EMTs arrived, they noted that my heart rate had bottomed out at 18, and at 18 beats per minute, you're basically dead.)

When I died, what I felt was energy, a constantly connected, beautiful and fantastic energy. There was no time, place, or space, and nothing to see, except a kind of electric, two-way vision made from strands of that inconceivable energy, like the whipping lines of cars' taillights photographed by a time-lapse camera. I was in space: no sound, no wind, nothing save this extraordinary electricity by which I am connected to everybody and anything, anyone and everything. I am in every given moment, in one instant, magnified to a number ungovernable by math.

What came to me on that ice was an exhilarating peace, the most profound adrenaline rush, yet an entirely tranquil one at the same time: electric serenity. I can still feel that space, silent, still, empty, but filled with every instant and all the forevers and, for the first time ever, my existence has nothing to do with time. It was an entirely beautiful place, filled with a knowable magic. It pulses; it floats; it is beyond language, beyond thought, beyond reason, a place of pure feeling.

I could see my lifetime. I could see everything all at once. It could have been for ten seconds; could have been for five minutes. Could have been forever. Who knows how long? In that death there was no time, no time at all, yet it was also all time and forever.

All life was grand; all life just got better in death. Everything and everyone I love or ever loved in my life was with me. Remember when you were a kid at Disneyland or it was Christmas morning, and you feel that jangly, super-excitement in your blood? It was that feeling to a degree immeasurable. I saw light strands, too, strands that connected me visually to everything, always, forever. I believe all energy is always connected; there's no time continuum there. This death confirmed this for me: I was nowhere, in a nonlinear energy land filled with beauty and wonder.

I knew then, as I know now to this day and will always know: Death is not something to be afraid of.

I'm really excited about living, of course, but death? It's not something I'm scared of anymore. I was never all that afraid of it before the incident, to be honest, but now I know that death is something to look forward to, a return to that electric serenity outside of time.

To me death is a confirmation of life, something always connected and eternal. It is not dark, not the end, not a disaster—it is magnificent, and exhilarating; it is your soul, and your love, concentrated into

their purest forms. Dying, you become connected to the collective energy everywhere all at once, which is itself a kind of divinity. And it is a
fierce teacher. Dying I learned the futility and temporary nature of hatred,
ranged as it is against the permanence of love. Though fear and hatred are
the flashiest and sometimes the most powerful human emotions, they are
merely the hare facing off against the tortoise of love. Love slowly, quietly,
and patiently waits for hate to simply burn out. It requires so much more
energy to hate than to love, and love has all the time in the world.

The only way love wins is across a span of time—it's not an instant
fix to anything, but it always wins. Let's imagine that you've hated somebody in your life—we all have at some point. Years later, do you still
burn with that hatred? Probably not. It's pretty much impossible to hate
so passionately across a span of many years; hate burns hot and fast, it's
flashy, and it can seem like the purest answer to injustice, but its heat
ruins hope as it foments more hatred, more conflicts, more wars. But hate
and fear burn out—they can't win in the end. And after death, none of
this matters anyway; hate won't outlive anyone—only love can do that.

I could not have prepared for the kind of catastrophe that I'd just
gone through on the ice; I don't think any of us knows what's in store.
How could we?

And on the ice, lying there newly as a man who had died, those
choices and struggles I'd been through, those fears I'd faced and con-
quered, all of it came together to fuel my ability to not only return from
death but to also bring with me some cheat codes, some messages, some
keys to life.

No experience need be wasted. Everything that happens to us can
be stored as information so that when disaster strikes, we don't curl up
and stop breathing. Instead, we find a position in which breathing is
possible. Then with all our strength we take that first, crucifying, agonizing breath. Groaning, we exhale, rasping into the icy air so that we
know we have exhaled (feel free to curse as you do so—I found it helped
me). Then, we fight through every impulse to give up, and we draw in a
second, agonizing breath. Groaning, we exhale . . . on, and on, and on,

until we lose strength, perhaps, and fade into the unknown, until something in us—who knows what?—grabs us by the soul and drags us back into life, where with all our strength once again we start to breathe.

*   *   *

Our experiences on earth have little to zero value after death; our DNA is merely the physical code for our bodies, then atoms to cosmic dust, what we bequeath and leave behind, but our spirit remains eternal, free of disease, or addiction, or pain, or time.

Anybody could have gone through what I went through—perhaps not the exact incident I had, as I will always believe it was a complete one-off, a cosmic fluke—but people have catastrophic accidents all the time. The exact coordinates of the disaster matter not, it's what one does with the information that comes with the experience that matters. And if, like me, someone has faced their death head-on, what's learned in those moments should cajole us into living our time more fruitfully on this planet. And that's a lesson for all of us, not just those of us lucky enough to have come back from the dead.

There is so much nonsense going on in the world right now, tremendous amounts of damaging white noise. We are all sucked into it, through those little computers we carry around with us in our pockets, machines whose algorithms force us to bear silent witness to catastrophes all around the globe constantly, even when there's nothing we can do about them except be drawn down into a caldera of depression and inertia. But when faced with the tumult of incidents—the wars and betrayals, the losses and disasters, amplified as they are by the inanity of social media, and underpinned by the need for everyone everywhere to be speaking at all times (as Bo Burnham puts it, "Is it necessary that every single person on this planet expresses every single opinion that they have, on every single thing that occurs, all at the same time?")—something like living beyond death incinerates so much of what is ancillary. What happened that day, and since, has made me want to oversimplify everything or, more exactly, recognize what's simple about the simple things. I think about my breath; that's all I had to do that day, breathe. Everything else would have been white noise.

And death doesn't need to be an ending—I don't believe in "afterlife" because life to me is an always and continuous thing. The only death is the death of the body, and the "worst thing" that can happen in your life, which so many of us think is death, is actually the best thing that will happen to us because we are then freed, relieved of our earthly burdens of "gravity, time, and tooth decay." Allow the rest to fall into ego, meaningless things. Taxes, a parking ticket, the stresses of an incorrect Starbucks order? All is just garbage-nonsense. In dying, we're relieved of those and *all* burdens. The best thing that can happen in our lives is to be relieved of all the randomness, the good and the bad of an afternoon. We might buy a winning lottery ticket or get a promotion at our company or win an Oscar, but none of these things are the ultimate truth. The continuance of the spirit is what is true, and things that are truthful are love. The only thing that matters in life is love. Love, here on earth, is our only currency; it is our energy and our existence, and we take that energy with us into perpetuity. We use words to communicate and data and satellites to connect to people . . . but we don't, not really. We're always connected by love if we allow it to be so, because our energies are free of the sublunary world.

All this I discovered when I died on the ice.

And something else: Dying has left me with this simple but imperative thought: Live your life *now*. Do the best you can with what you have now, but don't fear death, because even if you come back and your body is busted, there is still a sea of faces peering down at you, urging you to survive. I can see them still, innocently waiting up at the house, waiting for me to take them on a ski day . . . as I died I saw Ava, and Meemaw, and my dad, and Kym, and Nicky, and Kayla, and Dave, and Rory, and all my other siblings and friends, their faces ranged against death, urging me back, urging me to breathe, to struggle, to not let go.

Don't let go . . .

. . . these were the thoughts I had as I drifted back to Alex and Barb and Rich, back onto the asphalt, back to the ice, and blood, and trauma, and a working left eye hanging out of its socket.

*   *   *

What I'd just been through—my death—proved to me something I'd always intuited, which is that whatever we are goes beyond our galaxies, and it keeps going, repeating to the nth degree. I believe I was the recipient of something like a divine intervention, but I also like to think that in facing my fears, in knowing my body as I did, in being clear about what I wanted in life, and what I didn't want, and in finding my next breath, meant that in some ways I was built to push myself to a place where I could receive that intervention. I think this mixture of genetics and mental acuity, the emotional and mental effort from all those years of fighting my fears . . . it all coalesced to me knowing, deep in my soul, that if I'd panicked, my death would have been absolute, not fleeting, and that I could face this ultimate fear and struggle my way back from physical oblivion. If I passed out completely, I would've died forever. So I didn't allow myself to fully pass out. I felt like my struggles through the years had created in me the ability to face ultimate adversity, and hopefully to overcome, but I didn't know what I could truly overcome until I was tested to my limits and then beyond.

How do you really know until you're really tested?

I find it fascinating to look at the structure of a cell in our body. A nucleus at the center, with protons, neutrons, and electrons bouncing all around it. Similarly, the structure of that tiny cell, so crucial to life, mimics the solar system we are in. The sun takes the role of the nucleus, just as the planets and moons take the place of the protons, neutrons, etc. Then, zooming out to our galaxy, that structure is then seemingly repeated beyond our comprehension.

In everything, we can always control our perspective. We're all the authors of our own narrative. How we feel about things is down to us

and how we perceive things—it's our responsibility to control our perspective. We all have the capacity to captain our own ship. With permis-
sion to board the vessel, we now set our long course to press on with the
simple task of capturing the next breath.

My honest perception of the incident was, and is, and will always be,
that it was a *glory* moment. I didn't fucking die. So the celebration of the
New Year becomes a recognition of the depth of the love in our family.
And the snowcat is the bat signal for that love. Think of all the miracles I
received: I didn't *lose* any limbs or suffer any brain damage; there are no
permanent injuries to my spinal cord; most of my organs escaped lasting
effects, all of which is almost impossible to believe, given the power of
that machine and the relative fragility of the human form . . . What I
became instead was the recipient of three people on the ice caring for me
with all their hearts until paramedics could arrive.

But this didn't just happen to me. It could be easy to be victimized or
let the haunting images and the terror I caused dominate the rest of their
lives. Take Alex: He was with me the whole time. He'd had to sit and
stare at me dying on the ice, holding my arm, down on his haunches for
nearly forty-five minutes, his legs shaking once he finally got to stand, the
muscles taut and painful for days afterward. But he had no idea he had
been squatting at all—to keep me in a position in which I could properly
breathe, he literally couldn't move. He had to crouch there and hold my
arm in perfect stillness, ministering with pure love to me even though he
could have no idea if I'd survive. Before that he'd raised the alarm, which
had been a genius move because it revealed an intelligence that he knew
he couldn't do this on his own, and to leave me for an extended period
would have been tantamount to a death sentence. He did what he needed
to do, and he did it with unwavering love, a hero's love. And it wasn't as
if I'd always been easy on him; my role in his life was to be a mentor,
but one who challenged him and held him accountable, and that wasn't
always easy. I'm known in my family and circle of friends to give Renner
Talks, where I challenge people to improve, to commit harder, to face
their failings and be better, to not be afraid. There's no real upside for me

in giving a Renner Talk—no one wants to hear stripped-down truths, and often people don't know they even have these issues that I can see and that I am facing them with. There have been plenty of times people have said, "Who the fuck are you to tell me about my problems?" but I simply reply, "I'm only repeating back what *you* are telling *me*." When I stay with it, and when someone feels witnessed and understood, the seed of love is planted, and it makes it all worthwhile.

Alex had been the recipient of such Renner Talks multiple times, and I know I've challenged him often in ways that are really tough. But here he was, as committed as anyone ever could be in the face of death. He squatted with me, giving me life. And the images in that poor kid's brain . . . and yet it isn't entirely about what he had to witness. Every breath I took was a sign of him loving on me. I was drawing in that love and breathing it out. Without him, I'd have been fucking dead.

All that struggle was love and beauty to me. Eternal love cannot exist without suffering.

If you can look at it from that perspective, what happened that day— including my death—was a beautiful exchange of eternal love. It was also a sign that death is not invincible, nor need it be the final statement in the book of one's life.

Love: That's what lasts. That's what wins. Always.

*　　*　　*

Something in me pulled me out of death. I don't know what; I'll never know what. Barb later said, "There was something in him, something he managed to pull out of himself, and he just came back."

And when I come back, I feel a kind of a vague disappointment. Now all I have are these inadequate words to try to explain what happened . . . oh, and now I'm also back in this twisted, broken body?

I realize that I'm getting colder, and my breathing remains a physical torment unlike any other I've ever faced. (Back from death once, I wonder now if I could have beaten it a second time.) I am severely hypothermic, and my pain is unutterable, and every breath is still being chiseled out of stone so dense as to be almost impermeable.

And then, perhaps ten minutes after I died, in the very distance of my mind I hear sirens, can hear the whooshing of helicopter blades (though they could have been angel's wings, or those of the devil, I suppose), though from the evidence of the 911 call, these things are my fevered, pain-altered imaginings.

DISPATCHER: They should be driving down right now.
RICH: I can see them . . . I just saw them come through the trees.
  . . .
DISPATCHER: I did advise him that it's very icy roads coming down from that part of the hill as well.
RICH: I'll walk up there and tell them to slow down a little bit just in case . . . [Another accident] would be horrible. I don't hear any sirens.
DISPATCHER: They're in the area trying to locate . . . We're on the phone with the fire truck right now. They're coming down right now, it looks like.

Then as I continue to heave my breathing into the frozen morning, I feel the very air around me change as Alex and Barb and Rich's various energies shift, as though some part of this great burden is at last about to be shared, at last about to be borne by others, lifted momentarily. Through the fog of breath and pain I can hear new voices, and then the rustle of starched uniforms, someone's saying, "He's at eighteen, he's at eighteen," which they must have construed as me being seconds from death, though they could now know that I had already been through death and had broken back through the veil, returned to the ice and the asphalt and the breathing and the fourteen ribs sticking through my skin, my left eye alert and free, seeing everything and nothing.

To all of us—to me, to Alex, to Barb, to Rich—it had felt like a life-time, but now here was a fire engine. (Rich's 911 call alone lasted nearly twenty minutes.) The paramedics had parked up the hill a little ways, and Barb remembers thinking, *Why are you guys taking so long? It felt like they just were getting out of the truck so slowly, but then by that point everything was in slow motion . . .* Nothing is quick enough when you are surrounded by trauma. Somewhere in the distance a helicopter continues to circle, trying to find somewhere safe to land amid all that snow.

As the first three paramedics step in, Alex, Barb, and Rich retreat a little to give the professionals space to work. For Barb, it felt like a newly terrible moment.

"He was my kid right then," she said later. "Though I knew he was in good hands with the paramedics, it was so hard to let him go."

*   *   *

Meanwhile, Dave Kelsey had taken a brief nap, eaten some breakfast, and had headed back out to clear more snowmobiles and vehicles. His own car was parked down at the end of the driveway near Barb and Rich's house—with the weather deteriorating when he'd arrived a few days earlier, he figured it was a safer bet to leave his car on the road rather than try to navigate the curving, hilly driveway, so he decided to see if he could dig it out. One of the snowmobiles was now fully freed and parked in the driveway so he jumped on it and headed down toward the main road.

As he reached the final turn, he saw a helicopter hovering above the highway, and a bunch of fire trucks, red and blue lights flashing, and then the snowcat and the F-150 . . . and hurrying now, he saw Alex standing over me, but his brain didn't compute what his eyes were telling him.

"Oh, fuck," he told me he thought as he approached, "what happened to Alex? It must be Alex because Jeremy would never get hurt . . ." This, even though he was looking at Alex crouched over me holding my arm, me curled on my side.

The paramedics have already cut off some of my clothing to get easier access to me. Dave sees three guys working on me, and the terrible situation begins to dawn on him. Jumping off the snowmobile, he gets to work.

"Hey, how can I help?" he says.

"Who are you?" one of the paramedics says.

"I'm a dear friend . . ."

"Grab the tape," another paramedic says.

Dave starts pulling inch-long pieces off the tape and sticking them to his hand. The paramedics are putting a second IV in me by this point, and as they work, Dave takes my hand in his. He looks at me so intensely; I look back at him and squeeze his thumb. Dave seems so calm; he knows me to be an empath, a caregiver for everybody else, and I think he wanted to signal to me that at that moment the role was reversed, if only temporarily. As he put it later, "You're always the guy, but you were not the guy right then. I wanted your energy to be one hundred percent focused on your own life and not be worried about me. If you needed to lean on me spiritually, energetically, emotionally, then I had to show you that I was solid."

Dave does everything he can to exude strength for me.

"Hey, buddy," he says, maintaining a fierce eye contact as the paramedics continue to work to stabilize me and get me out of pain, "you're doing great. You just keep breathing. You got this."

I have been manually breathing for nearly forty-five minutes by this point, and I am exhausted, fading in and out of consciousness. But through the fog of the pain and the exercise of bringing air into shattered lungs I hear my mind say, "They're here." As the paramedics had gotten to work, as they'd first cut off some of my clothes, and as their voices swirled around me, it was right then I knew that I had to give my body to them. I had nothing left at that moment, no more hope of walking back to the house, no more belief that the cramps would go away, no more thoughts of taking the kids skiing. No more Epsom salts bath.

Help was here, and I knew I had to surrender, give them my body to do as they needed.

I don't find myself in this position often, but right then that morning

I give up everything to them. For one of the first times in my life, I am willing to be saved by others. This doesn't happen much for me—I like to do things on my own. In fact, I'd always been known for being pretty terrible at receiving help; the mere offer of it could even make me angry at times. I had always loved the challenge of overcoming something without anyone's help.

But here on the ice it was time to let go. I didn't know it then, but this would set the tone for my recovery in the next weeks and months; there was so much I couldn't do without help, and I learned to ask for it. But that was all to come—for now, I didn't even have the strength to ask, and I was far from out of the woods.

As he holds my gaze, Dave notices that my face is again turning a strange color—he described it later as like watching a fish, or a lizard, slip from green to yellow to orange. He takes a quick glance over at the heart monitor the paramedics had attached to my chest and is horrified to watch it precipitously dropping—from 90 and 80, it has cratered to below 50. Dave looks back at me; he doesn't let on what he's seen, but he told me later that he subtly motioned to one of the paramedics that my heart rate was dangerously low—by this point it was 38, which is critical.

The paramedics also realize that because my chest wall is so compromised, my breathing so labored, my oxygen so low that they will have to pierce my chest cavity to release the pressure. Doing so brings immediate relief.

Still the helicopter struggles to find somewhere to land; winds are still gusty this morning, and there really isn't a suitable place big enough to accommodate the bird. Rich's suggestion that they land at the Tanenbaum Event Center had been a good one, but it hadn't worked out; it would take a few more minutes before the helicopter finally finds a safe place to land on the frozen Mount Rose Highway. (This had been a crucial call by Barb to tell Rich to ask for a helicopter—later that day it would take people an hour or more to get down the hill and to the hospital because of the almost impassable roads between my house and Reno.)

A flurry of new and even more focused activity begins; I was told later that paddles were retrieved from the ambulance in case they needed to jolt my heart, but before they can use them on me, a red body board appears. The paramedics had been keeping me as stable as possible while the helicopter found a place to land, but now that it was on the ground, the board would be used to get me to the ambulance, and then to the bird as quickly as possible.

Dave says, "There's a board here, Jeremy. We're going to put you on it and we're going to get you in the ambulance, and then you've done it. You got this."

Dave and the paramedics manage to get me on the board and shuffle along the icy road to the ambulance. I hear the body board click into place and then I'm raised into the truck. Safe in the back of the ambulance, I am driven down the road to the CareFlight helicopter, whose blades continued to whir on the highway, readying me for the short flight to Reno.

*   *   *

From this point on New Year's Day until sometime on January 3, my memory is mostly blank. I was deeply sedated for the journey to the hospital, in triage, in the ICU, and for the initial surgeries I went through. Necessarily this account of those days draws heavily upon the memories of my family and friends, each of whom went through their own trauma, but all of whom stepped up in extraordinary ways for me, for my daughter, and for each other.

*   *   *

Once the ambulance had driven away, Dave noticed that the paramedics who had been left behind seemed to look almost scared about what they'd seen. One of them quietly said to his colleague, "Do you know who that was? It was Jeremy Renner," and Dave was moved by the vulnerable humanity and profound shock each displayed once their extraordinary lifesaving efforts were over.

By this point the sheriff's department had also arrived and had started to question Alex about what had happened. Alex told me later that the first cop he spoke to seemed like a rookie, "a guy who didn't quite fit his uniform yet," as Alex joked. He set about asking Alex to fill out an accident report—frustrated and traumatized, my nephew remembers writing, "Alex Freeze; [phone number]; [birthday]; Jeremy Renner got run over by a snowcat; accident," and signed it. Fortunately, Dave noticed that Alex was being peppered with questions and seemed uncomfortable with the process and hurried across the ice to take over the interview. Motioning to the snowmobile, Dave told Alex to ride it back to the house to tell his mom what had happened.

"Don't wake anybody up," Dave said to Alex. "Don't tell anybody what happened—just go get your mom. Go slow. And Alex, all I want you to do is breathe. Just focus and breathe."

As Alex started back to the house, Dave—realizing that the twenty or so people in the house would soon learn of the accident and would subsequently and quickly need to get out of Camp Renner and to the hospital—started to try to break up the ice to clean up the blood, which was everywhere. And there were some of my clothes to collect, too, which Dave started to put in a bag. Dave really didn't want the family to see anything . . . especially Ava. But as he did so, he was asked by the sheriff's department to desist. They told him that this whole area was still a potential crime scene. Rich and Barb, who had by now done everything they could have done and more, handed Dave my phone before they headed back to their house.

Barb told me later that the rest of the day was very painful for her and Rich—for a start she had a lot of blood on her that needed cleaning up, and going through all this not twenty-four hours after seeing her uncle on his deathbed left her shattered. But beyond that, they had both been through a significant trauma. As I've said, this incident didn't happen just to me, and as bad as it was about to be for my family when they found out what had occurred, Barb and Rich went through something terrifying, too. Given the severity of what they'd just witnessed, it was no surprise that they privately agreed it was "going to be a miracle" if I survived.

For months afterward Barb had bad nightmares about that day. She'd wake up and be haunted by the image of me just lying there on the driveway . . . and the sound of someone dying is, in her words, "just one of the worst sounds. You can't even imagine." Even months later Barb, her chickadee feeders at every window signaling the size of her heart, still wells up with tears when she talks about that morning.

*   *   *

The reverberations of the incident went beyond even what I could ever have imagined. For a start, less than half a mile from my house Kym was about to be told what had happened, and Alex couldn't know it but it would release a tsunami into the lives of our family.

It was still the most beautiful morning imaginable. As Alex rode back up the driveway toward the house, he looked out to his left, where the sun was just coming up, right over the crest. There was not a cloud in sight—he realized he hadn't seen the sky in two or three days. Everything was shiny; everything was glistening; for a moment it could be imagined that nothing was out of place, nothing terrible had happened, no one had been critically injured just a half mile from this scene of natural beauty.

Alex thought, *If he's going to die, this is what it looks like.* He was nearing the house and began to wonder what those five seconds of telling his mother were going to be like. What was everybody feeling right before they found out what had happened? Did anybody know already? Alex had no idea what to expect, and he really didn't know how to say anything to anybody. But he knew he had to tell his mom, and quickly.

How do you describe what had happened that morning on the driveway? Knowing how much love there was in this family, and how central to everyone's lives his uncle was, Alex was already at a loss for the right thing to say.

He parked the snowmobile and walked into the house. People were laughing; Rory was being his usual silly, goofy self, making people giggle as he tried to figure out the coffee machine and made a breakfast for people as they started to appear in the kitchen.

Alex saw his mom standing by the stove.

"Hey, Mom," Alex said, "can I talk to you for a minute?"

"Sure," she said. "You good?"

"Can we just talk outside, please?"

Alex and his mom slipped outside. Fortunately, they didn't catch anybody's attention; Alex remembers being grateful for that, at least.

"What's going on?" Kym said. "Everything good?"

Alex looked at his mom. He knew how close my sister and I are, how much we loved each other, how much we'd been through together. What could he possibly say?

"No, Mom," Alex said.

And then he told her what had happened.

"I don't know if he's going to survive, Mom," Alex said.

With those words hanging in the cold morning air, my nephew and my sister began to cry together. And that's also when their own recovery started, right there in the garage of Camp Renner, on New Year's Day, 2023.

6

OPERATION EVACUATION

While I was being flown to the Renown Regional Medical Center in downtown Reno, a Herculean effort of evacuation was just starting at Camp Renner.

To start with, Kym wanted to get to the hospital as quickly as possible, but she had to prep people for what had happened and organize getting everybody off the mountain before the next storm hit (more bad weather was in the forecast). Most especially, she had to work out how to deal with Ava—what to tell her, and what *not* to tell her.

With me still in the air, there was scant information about whether I was going to survive, so it was imperative for the family to make sure that Ava at least had the opportunity to get to me in case I wasn't going to make it. But there was a delicate balancing act in play, too. No one wanted to freak Ava out unnecessarily in case my long-term prognosis was a hopeful one.

I don't know what I would have done in that situation, but the solutions my family came up with on the fly that morning epitomize both the depth of their love and their brilliance in the face of a logistical nightmare and family crisis.

*   *   *

My sister Kym was the superstar who initially took the reins of this disaster and created sense out of it, shared information when she could, and made sure my care was as good as it could be.

But to begin with she, too, had to learn how to breathe.

When she had woken that first morning of 2023, the first things Kym noticed had been the distant sound of a helicopter. She figured the news teams were airborne covering the extent of the historic weather event we'd all just been through. But with the weather clearing, and the vehicles clear of the drifts, she also knew it was going to potentially be a busy day getting everyone ready to head to the slopes, and there was no time to lie around. Pulling on her T-shirt, she headed downstairs where she found Rory and a couple of the kids hanging out and goofing around; otherwise, it was quiet at Camp Renner.

Rory said, "The coffee's flowing, get yourself a cup. We've been up all morning digging cars out."

As they chatted, at first Kym hadn't noticed Alex enter the house. But he came up behind her and whispered that he needed to talk to her. She was confused because Alex had kept his boots on—this was a strict no-no in a house with white carpets. But she could tell by her son's countenance that something was up—she figured he'd maybe wrecked one of my vehicles. *He's rolled it*, she thought, *and he's freaking out and he doesn't know how to tell Jeremy.* But as ever with Kym, her next thought was, *We will problem-solve; we will figure this out.*

Out in the garage, she realized Alex was out of breath, almost hyperventilating, clearly traumatized by something. What could it possibly be?

And then he started telling her exactly what had happened.

"There's been an accident, Mom," he said through shallow breaths. "The snowcat ran over Jeremy. He got caught. Mom, his eye was out . . ."

All the while, Kym kept interrupting him.

"Just hold on, Mom," Alex said, desperate to tell her everything he could. "His eye's out, Mom, everything's crushed. He wasn't breathing. They got him on a helicopter, they airlifted him. I don't even know if he's still breathing, Mom, I really don't know anything."

It's incredible how a traumatized mind reacts: Kym's immediate thoughts were, *I need to get a bra on because I don't have a bra on, and I have to get my keys, and I need a charger.*

To Alex she said simply, "I've got to go save my brother, I got to go and protect him."

Kym ran into the house, tears pouring down her face; Rory noticed and followed her upstairs. She told him she'd talk to him in the garage.

Upstairs, Kym told her partner, Frank, as much as she knew (and urged him to keep the information close to his chest) and grabbed her stuff.

"Please tell nobody because I don't want any kids to freak out," she said to Frank. "Don't say shit to anybody. No kids."

She put a bra on, and her shoes and a jacket, got her phone, her charger, and her purse, and headed to the garage, where she knew there was at least some cell service. Rory came to join her; she was uncontrollably weeping by this point. She said, "Jeremy's been run over. It's a terrible accident. He looks dead. And if he's going to make it, I've got to get people down to the hospital right away."

Rory went numb; being horrified and devastated by this terrible news about his best friend was bad enough, but it also very naturally took him back to the worst day of his life before that day.

Some forty years earlier, Rory's younger brother by two years, John, had been playing ice hockey two days before St. Patrick's Day, when he had been paralyzed after a brutal collision during a game in Canada. When it happened, Rory had been out of the country, and when he'd received the call, he'd collapsed in agony, only waking up a full two days later. He had always felt responsible for his younger brothers and remembers thinking that he was the one who was to blame for what had happened to John. *Why didn't I prevent it?* he remembers thinking. *Where were you?* Rory had felt helpless for years, and with the news that morning in the garage, instantly a whole host of suppressed feelings of guilt and uselessness returned. But the news also made him realize that he had an important job to do. His task would be to make smoothies and coffee and food, to make people laugh in these, the most difficult of circumstances, and do anything else that was needed to make sure this family he loved were able to deal with what would be terrible days ahead.

But Ava—what to do about Ava? She was not yet awake, but when she did finally get up it would be crucial to handle her with care. The problem for Rory was that he's an honest salesman, uncomfortable with—and therefore terrible at—lying. His gut was roiling but he knew he had to put on the Rory show, however bad he was at dissembling.

Rory got his first test almost immediately: Ava was finally awake, and as ever the first thing she always wants to do when she jumps out of bed in the morning is find me.

"Where's my dad?" she said to Rory.

"Oh, I'm not sure, honey, but don't worry," Rory said. "Here, have some eggs."

Rory knew that I'd want him to do one thing above all else: protect my child from the situation until we knew what was going on. If I was going to make it, then there was no need to worry her just yet. If I was going to die, then that information would need to come from my mom or from Ava's mom.

Rory loves Ava as though she's one of his own; I love his kids the same way. And we'd always discussed that if anything ever happened to either of us, our families would be our first line of defense, and that we'd always take care of each other's kids as a priority. So that morning Rory knew he had a role, a job to do, a purpose, which would ultimately be healing for him because when his brother had been so badly injured all those years earlier, he had felt, as he put it, "like a fly in a hurricane." But still, it was so painful to have to lie to Ava.

"We'll go see him later," Rory said, secretly praying this was no lie.

*　　*　　*

Meanwhile, Kym knew she had to call our mom and tell her what had happened.

The only problem was, they weren't on speaking terms and hadn't been for months—Kym wasn't sure if Mom would even pick up.

Fortunately, Mom answered immediately when she saw it was Kym. What came next was later described by Mom as "the worst phone call she'd ever received in her entire life."

"Mom," Kym said, "something happened. Jeremy got into an accident—"

But before Kym could continue, Mom started screaming.

"Shut up, stop it, don't say it, Kym," she yelled. "Stop it!"

"Mom," Kym said, desperate to convey as much as she could before she headed down the mountain, "I'm not going to have cell service for an hour. I'm heading down the road. I don't know what's going on. But you got to get up here."

Then she said, "Mom, he wasn't breathing. And his eye was out . . ."

Mom was stuck in Modesto and wasn't sure how she was going to make it to Reno, but for now, Kym's priority was to get to me as soon as possible. After she called our dad and filled him in, too, Alex appeared to tell his mom that someone was waiting to meet her at the bottom of the driveway right by where the incident had happened. She would need help to get out of the area because the roads were still closed, and one of the firefighters had agreed to drive her to Reno.

Nobody talk to me, Kym thought. *Just let me breathe. Let me stay focused.* She had gone into what she later described as shock-and-fix-it mode. But mostly she realized that she, too, had actually stopped breathing, or at least had forgotten to remember to breathe.

Alex took his mom down the driveway on a snowmobile where they found the kindly firefighter waiting to drive her to Reno. At the scene of the incident Kym was pleased to not see much blood, but there were still tons of lights and vehicles everywhere—in fact, she didn't quite know what she was seeing. Like Dave Kelsey before her, my sister couldn't process the scene at all.

A firefighter captain drove her away from Camp Renner but, probably wanting to avoid any more disasters, he drove incredibly slowly—despite the break in the storm, the roads were still treacherous. Kym knew the captain was just being safe, but she really wanted to yell at him. *You can't go this slow*, she thought. *I need to be there. I need to be there. I need to be there.* She had no one to call, no one to text. The weight of the story was on her—on her and Alex and David Kelsey and Frank and Rory, but for now the burden of the unforeseen fell on her harder than anyone.

At some point on the way to Reno, Kym got service and called Dad. He had been very subdued when Kym had called him; he, too, was in deep shock. And he was faced with a hell drive from Grass Valley, too, ninety miles southwest of Reno. He'd have to make it through the Yuba Pass, a 6,700-foot elevation highway that had already seen multiple cars break down and be abandoned in the great snows—but nothing was going to stop my dad getting to me.

Mom, on the other hand, was unsure how she'd ever make it. Another storm was coming, the only flight available arrived in Reno four days into the new year, and all the other flights were already being canceled or were fully booked. The roads remained either dangerous or impassable. And then, a stroke of good fortune: My brother Kyle's sister-in law, who had also been visiting to celebrate the new baby, announced that she and her husband would be riding back to Reno that very day to beat the next storm, and in a huge truck with chains on the tires no less. It was the obvious and very fortunate fix for my mom's predicament. The three of them set off almost immediately, not even pausing once for a food or pee break all the way east. But the usual route they'd take, 99 north to Sacramento (before heading east on I-80), was flooded in parts, so they'd had to divert over to the 5 freeway to get up to 80, and because everyone else had had the same idea, it took more than thirteen hours to make a trip (Modesto to Reno) that usually takes just over three.

Kym's drive to Reno wasn't as long as our parents' respective trips, but still she was in a personal hell. She didn't really know anything—the image of my eye out of my skull haunted her, as it haunted my mother on her trip, too—and she just wanted to scream. Eventually, after about an hour she finally made it to the private back entrance of Renown Regional Medical Center. Kym didn't know which of her personalities was going to show up. Was she going to freak out, or just kick into her default professional setting—she's a boss, very task oriented, a fixer—and ask a shit ton of questions?

The first person she ran into was a dear friend of mine, a former firefighter with the Truckee Meadows Fire and Rescue, Jesse Corletto. Jesse and I had met when Jesse had been renovating a 1930s building in Reno—I'd shown up to discuss the architecture and the project generally and we'd become fast friends.

On New Year's Day, Jesse had been building snow ramps in his yard for his eight-year-old son when he had gotten a call from one of his former colleagues who knew that Jesse and I were close friends.

"Hey, thought you should know that we just responded to a scene," Jesse's colleague said. "It was Jeremy. It's pretty bad. He was loaded into a helicopter."

Then he said words that caused Jesse's heart to stop.

"We did the best we could, Jesse," he said. "Just wanted you to know."

"We did everything we could" is EMT code for a lost cause; Jesse knew that. With those words echoing in his mind, he'd rushed to the hospital, as had nine or ten other firefighters and first responders. As part of the *Rennervations* TV show, I'd repurposed an ambulance and donated it back to the community, so I was well known in the area. By the time Kym arrived, there was a small group of guys waiting at the back door. Kym had naturally been startled by the crowd of first responders waiting there—she knew that medical professionals do a really good job at hiding stuff from people, but seeing all of my friends she instantly figured there was something terrible that she hadn't yet been told.

In the hospital, Kym headed straight to the reception desk, but when she said my name, the sweet woman just said, "Oh, a social worker will be right out to speak with you."

Kym, once again fearing the worst, started crying again, but Jesse stepped in. It was so difficult for him because he felt so helpless; every trauma he'd ever worked on had affected him, but when it was a friend and he hadn't gotten to help directly, he felt extra lost. But even though he figured the news was going to be catastrophic, given the call he'd received and what that phrase "we did the best we could" usually meant, he wasn't about to let on to my sister.

"Hey, that's not what you think it means, Kym," Jesse said. "Just hold on. We don't know anything yet."

Almost instantly Kym's phone rang—a 775 number, which was local. It was the ER doctor.

"Jeremy's stable," he said. "We have him up in the ICU and the social worker's coming to take you up there."

Kym took a deep, deep breath, and headed upstairs.

*   *   *

When she arrived at the ICU, Kym found everybody looking at her: a mix of sympathy and sorrow and condolence.

"Come this way," someone said.

Kym walked into the ICU, and there I was. She fell to pieces, to see her brother, usually so strong but now so helpless. I was attached to wires and lines; I was bloodied, comatose, my face a mess. By this point my eye had been taped back into place, but still the signs of bodily trauma were obvious and deeply distressing to her. The room was baking hot, but my skin was stone cold.

Kym put her hand on my arm.

He's dead, she thought. *He's dead.*

She turned to one of the nurses.

"Is he going to make it?" she said.

"I'm sorry," the nurse said. "We'll get someone who can talk to you."

For the next four hours, when she wasn't dealing with doctors and their plans for me, Kym was with me alone. Though I was comatose, she'd remembered that even through a coma it's thought that people can hear you, so she kept talking.

"You're so strong," she said, "you're going to be just fine. Mom's on her way, Dad, too. Ava is fine. The kids are okay. Everyone's on their way."

As she sat there, a stream of doctors cycled through, but Kym was frustrated that she couldn't get a clear, full picture. One doctor would talk about my leg, another about my lungs and my ribs, another about my breathing, another one yet about my eye. I was briefly brought out of sedation at one point, and they made me move a toe and squeeze Kym's finger—this signaled that my brain was probably working okay, but that was all Kym knew, and she also knew that I wouldn't want to live if I was a vegetable. These were the decisions that were in her hands, like it or not. She was a fixer, yes, but perhaps some things would be beyond her magic.

Every few minutes she'd call Mom and fill her in on what was happening. For her part, it never crossed my mom's mind that I would die. Though the visual of my eye being ripped out of my head haunted her, she still never thought she needed to hurry up before she lost me— she just knew she had to get to me, but incredibly she always believed I'd survive.

Amid all the decisions about my care that Kym was having to make, my dad arrived. She remained in fix-it mode, living off adrenaline. She thought to take tons of pictures, just in case, and she was happy to see, too, that every time she covered my foot up with the blanket, I'd somehow kick it off—she didn't know that's how I sleep (I can't stand my feet being covered), but I guess something in my life spirit was yet again forging its way to the surface.

Elsewhere, my sister Nicky had secured a flight to Reno from LA that would arrive that evening and had also thought to book as many hotel rooms as possible for everyone who had been at Camp Renner. With more bad weather approaching, and no idea how long I'd be in the hospital, it was a great act of foresight.

Frank had already gotten Ava and Kym's youngest daughter, Bella, off the mountain and down to an arcade where he gave them as much money as possible to distract them, while doing everything he could to keep their phones away from them. Already the news of the incident had begun to filter out, and Frank knew that Bella, especially, who is older than Ava by a few years, would be checking her phone if it was within reach.

Back at Camp Renner, Dave Kelsey had led the charge to evacuate, putting people on task. My brother Clayton was there with his newborn and he'd announced he was just going to put his baby on his shoulders and hike out; fortunately, Dave nixed that idea, and Clayton and the baby were the first to be taken down to the main road. Then, Frank had left with Ava and Bella; Jesse eventually arrived with his truck to move all the suitcases; refrigerators were emptied, doors locked. By the time Dave's car was pulled out of a drift at the bottom of the driveway, right where the incident had happened, it was already getting dark, five thirty p.m.

The scene was eerily quiet. The lights were gone; most of the blood gone; just the snowcat sitting deep into the side of the F-150, a tableau reminding everyone of what had occurred hours earlier.

Off the mountain, most of the family went to hotel rooms, but Dave chose to drive his family back over the passes west, all the way home to Menlo Park. Dave and his family arrived home at about one in the morning; he'd already booked a flight back to Reno the next morning, but for now he just wanted to sleep in his own bed, his family safe in their beds, as though such a thing might mitigate a tiny bit of the horror of the day.

But each time Dave started to drift off, he would make it to the very edge of sleep before jumping awake, seeing my face, once again holding my hand.

Eventually he slept, dreaming of a wheat field. It was an image he'd once created for a meditation in an acting class, a class he and I had taken together many years earlier. The wheat field was way out in the country, great waving peals of yellow stalks, as though in a van Gogh painting, yet real, very real . . . a field of peace, still and alive, where Dave Kelsey could contemplate his place in the world.

But now, in the dream, in the distance there came the thrum of an engine, six sets of wheels turning, inexorable, powerful. What sounded like a snowplow was instead a thresher, and it was heading right for him. Nobody was driving it; Dave started to run, but the ground was ice, and he slipped, and waited, an eternity, trapped in this painting that was real, this true artifice, until he, too, felt the great power of a machine, the thresher passing over him until he was oblivion.

PART TWO

PATIENT

7

JENGA

Where am I?

I am floating in a place called Nowhere.

Who am I?

I am not Jeremy Renner, date of birth, 1.7.1971. For privacy reasons, I am "Banana Thirty-Eight," date of birth, "1.1.1900." I am drowning in a medically induced coma, so I may as well be Mr. Banana, the man with the silly name who turned 123 years old yesterday.

My face is swollen to such an extent that I could walk down any street and not be recognized—this would be a first, at least for the last twenty or so years. After *Dahmer*, after *The Hurt Locker*, and definitely after *Mission: Impossible* and the Marvel movies, my anonymity is a thing of the past.

But today, I am anonymous.

I am not Hawkeye, I am not Will James; I am not the Mayor of Kingstown; I'm not a product on a shelf, like hand soap.

Instead, I am a brother, a father, a son, and, more pressing, a code red patient on life support in an ICU.

My sister Kym stands above me and takes a photo. (I know none of this; I look at the photos months later.)

I am propped up in a hospital bed, a white sheet up to my neck. My head—the only part of me Kym could see—is tilted back, held in place by a white brace under my chin; it looks very uncomfortable, but I feel nothing. Under that sheet, more than thirty-eight broken bones, as well as various other injuries.

RIBS: six ribs broken, in fourteen places

PELVIS: three breaks in lower pelvis

RIGHT ANKLE: broken

LEFT LEG: tibia broken; spiral fracture

LEFT ANKLE: broken

RIGHT CLAVICLE: broken; dislocated

RIGHT SHOULDER BLADE: cracked; dislocated

FACE: eye socket, jaw, mandible, all broken

LEFT HAND: broken (Option for surgery was declined by Jeremy and doctor agreed with choice to let self-heal.)

LEFT WRIST: fractured

LEFT TOES: three breaks—two middle toes broken, left side of foot cracked (metatarsal)

OTHER

LUNG: collapsed and bruised

LIVER: pierced from rib bone

HEAD: major laceration back of head

RIGHT EARDRUM: damaged (?); can't hear

RIGHT KNEE: major strain (unknown extent of injury)

LEFT EYE: contusion and impact

I am intubated. There are one, two, three, four, five, six machines attached to me, belching out ever-changing numbers constantly: the lottery of my new existence, 125, 50, 95, 88/54, 98 . . . Drips slip their salving solutions along thin lines down over the edge of the top of the bed and on under the sheets to my veins. Everything is beige save the pistachio-colored blanket under my head and the luminous LED numbers ever changing.

My left eye betrays the trauma it so recently suffered. Though the eye is now back in the damaged socket, held in place by a white Band-Aid, the skin all around my eye and up into my brow is bruised a brutal smoky mauve, as though a makeup artist had lost his mind and just kept painting.

I had once been that makeup artist—it was a skill I'd learned by doing theater in college. When I left Modesto for Los Angeles, I was unknown, a young man with a paying job lined up with Lancôme cosmetics.

How far I had come until yesterday; now, who knows whether I'd need to start over.

*   *   *

Fame had made me something of a hermit. Knowing that as soon as I left the house I'd be recognized, I tended to hole up wherever I was. Certainly in Los Angeles—before the incident, I pretty much never left my house; I'd been living my life Covid-style before the virus hit (for about the last decade, in fact) and continued to do so even after the distance protocols were finally lifted. This was less true in Tahoe, where the sense of community is stronger and where people are more accepting of me as just a local guy. But when I did leave my house in LA, I was sometimes subject to what felt like relentless hounding. I would be just going about my day, at heart still just a small boy from a small town, and I'd try to always be very present with people, but sometimes that thoughtfulness would get taken advantage of. I never wanted to be rude to people; I knew I had to have a kind of politician face on to be out in public.

Sometimes, though, I wouldn't have my tolerance tank full—I'd just be picking up some sausages at the supermarket or some medication at the pharmacy, and not really in the mood to engage. Still, there were people who had bought the DVD or rented the movie or gone to the theater who thought they owned a bit of me, too, and that I owed them some of my time as a result. Sometimes this sense of entitlement would show up at a urinal or when I was in the middle of dinner with my daughter, and the cell phones would come out and start recording (this was a particular problem at urinals).

The comatose me didn't know that this was all about to change. A new relationship was about to be forged between me and the world. The days of the vampires were over.

But to even discover that, first I had to get out of this damn coma.

*   *   *

Ever since the helicopter had flown me away from the scene of the accident, I had been mostly unconscious.

The plan for my short- and long-term survival was to first address anything life-threatening. With a trauma as profound as the one I'd just been through, doctors first focus on what's most crucial to saving a life, creating a kind of pecking order for treatment—what's essential, what can wait—then piece together a plan from there. Sometimes it takes a few days, so all Kym and my father (and eventually my mom) knew was that the surgeries I had on New Year's Day were simply to secure my survival.

The care plan had been written on a white board the previous day, when I'd been admitted.

Preferred name: Jeremy

MY FAMILY
Lee: dad

Valerie: mom

Kym: sister

MY GOAL FOR THE DAY

Rest+heal

Tests and procedures:

X-rays

Mobility and activity:

Bed rest

WHAT HELPS ME WITH MY PAIN

100mcg fentanyl

MY CARE TEAM

RN: Becky

MD: Juell Swanson

RT: Makaila

But the section titled "My discharge plan" was empty—no entries for "next level of care," or "depends on," or "expected date."

So much else happened the day I was admitted. I'd find out about all of it days, weeks, months later.

*   *   *

My niece Kayla, Alex's sister, and her partner Mark had been staying at the guesthouse across from the main house at Camp Renner. On the morning of January 1, Kayla had woken at around seven thirty to find beautiful, clear weather. As she opened the curtains she found a deep azure sky, gorgeous, piled snow obliterating cars, trees, the driveway . . . three, four feet. Insane! Mark and Kayla were giggling at the enormity of what the storm had left behind when her phone rang.

It was my sister Nicky—she was in Los Angeles with her husband.

"Hi!" Kayla said. "Happy New Year—"

"Kayla, what happened," Nicky said, interrupting, a croak in her voice.

Kayla was on high alert immediately.

"What do you mean, 'What happened?'" Kayla said.

"Jeremy got run over," Nicky said, starting to bawl.

"What the fuck? What do you mean? What the fuck?" Kayla couldn't get her head around what she was hearing.

Mark was looking intently at her.

"Where is everyone?" Kayla said to no one in particular.

As Kayla, imagining her uncle had been hit by a car or something, threw pants and a hoodie on, Nicky told her everything she knew.

My mom had called Nicky earlier and had been barely understandable through heavy sobs. Nicky thought that maybe something had happened to our grandmother who was old and now in memory care. The last person she would've thought anything bad happened to would be me—she knew I was careful, even with all my boats and Jet Skis and big machinery.

Eventually Mom was able to describe the little that she knew: She said I'd been run over by a vehicle.

To Nicky, this had sounded like the very worst thing imaginable. Had I been on a snowmobile and been hit by a car? As the terrible images had swirled in her head, her adrenaline had spiked, as it tended to do whenever she found herself in times of high stress. She didn't know what to do or think, so she decided to walk around her house to get all of that adrenaline out of her body.

Bad idea: Instead of calming herself, she managed to pass out. Fortunately, her ten-year-old daughter Daphne sat with her until she came to, and then called her father (he wasn't home at the time). Auggie, her son, did what many boys might do, bless him, which was miss the whole thing because he was in his bedroom on his iPad.

Coming to fully, Nicky had called Kayla. Suddenly, things made sense to Kayla. She and Mark had indeed heard a helicopter while they were waking up, and now, realizing what she'd heard, her anger boiled.

"Why the fuck did nobody come get me?" she said.

Staying on the phone with Nicky, Kayla started to run to the main house, but the snow was up to her waist, and she described it as like running through heavy water. She saw Frank coming up the hill, and he explained that her mom had just left on a snowmobile to get to the main road and then head to the hospital.

Then Kayla saw Alex. Her brother's face was pale, ghostly, had etched upon it everything he'd seen that morning. And Kayla recognized that he was in fight-or-flight mode.

"What do we need to do to get off this mountain?" she said to Alex, giving him something to refocus his mind.

In the house, Kayla, Frank, Rory, Dave, and Alex sat around working out what to do. The key thing was to be careful with Ava; they didn't know much, in any case, but they certainly didn't want to freak her out. One of our cousins and Frank decided that they were going to walk Bella and Ava off the other side of the mountain—avoiding the spot where the incident had taken place, just in case—to where one of the neighbors had a car they could use to go down to Reno. There, Frank could wait it out until everyone decided what to tell Ava.

While the house got packed up, every fifteen minutes Kayla would go to the spot in the house where she could get phone service to get updates from her mom. Every time Kym called was more heart-wrenching than the last.

"His eye popped out of his head," Kym would say, or, "His ribs are broken. They think maybe a lung is punctured."

Then, "We're not sure about his brain . . ."

And every fifteen minutes everyone would cry with the new information, and then just as quickly cycle back into fix-it mode. Kayla, especially, knew she needed to take special care of Alex, given what he'd been through, and given that she saw him crying off to the side now and then.

"Operation Evacuation," as they dubbed it, took all day, but by the evening Kayla was able to get off the mountain with everyone else, and she headed straight to see me.

Nicky had also arrived by that point, too, flying in from LA on about the last flight available. She remembers thinking that she just had to get to Reno because it might have been her last chance to say goodbye . . . Meanwhile, my mom had also arrived, finally joining my dad and the rest of the family.

Kayla was devastated by what she found in my hospital room. Seeing me intubated, comatose, frozen in time wrecked her. She didn't know what to do, but someone had said that they were pretty sure I could hear people, so through my coma, a lilting singing voice came, singing "Lean on Me":

When you're not strong

. . .

I'll help you carry on

Kayla was singing to me. To this day she has no idea why that song came to her; she felt it was the only thing she could do. She sat there for a while just holding my hand, crooning to me softly. Kym joined her, and together they cleaned the blood off me with baby wipes.

Out in the waiting room, everyone was sobbing. During the afternoon and evening, the medical staff would briefly bring me out of the deep anesthesia, bringing my numbers up, and would say, "Jeremy, can you move your left toe, Jeremy?" and from somewhere deep inside me a residual ability sent signals down my body and my toe would almost imperceptibly move. Or they'd ask me to squeeze a finger and again, though it was barely noticeable, I did indeed apply pressure.

"He listened!" Kym would say through tears. "Oh my God, he got it right, he squeezed." Or my eyes would flicker, again so briefly.

Kym would occasionally bring people in to see me, two at a time: Rory and Dave, Kayla and Mark, Nicky, Mom, Dad, switching back and forth so that everyone got some time. But each time Kym stepped away she panicked—she had been there all day. *I can't leave*, she thought, *I need to get back to him*. Her motherly instincts were deeply activated, even to the point of feeling a tinge of annoyance, like Barb had earlier that day, that she had to give me up for a short time and leave me to other people.

Out in the waiting room, my family created a small circle of chairs beneath walls decorated with huge photos of irises. They played Jenga to pass the time, drank Starbucks and Minute Maid juices by the gallon, but barely ate. Kayla sat rooted to her phone; my mom stared into a sorrowful, scared middle distance; Alex paced, still in the beanie he'd worn all day. Eventually, ten boxes of pizza arrived (they'd been sent by the mayor, Hillary Schieve). My mom and dad hammed it up for a picture holding a pizza each, but no one really felt much like joking.

When she'd first arrived, my mom had come into the room and, like everyone else, had been heartbroken at what she found. She'd already seen the state of me during a FaceTime call that Kym had organized, but seeing me in person was incredibly traumatic for her—especially my eye, which, though now taped (and the eyeball back in place), was still a sight she'll never get over. Months later she still cries when she describes it.

"To see your child there, to see it in person, was awful," she said to me recently. "And you were intubated, and your breathing was so terrible . . . The way it sounded . . ."

But my mom is all strength. She talked to me, telling me about her impossible trip from Modesto over the flooded passes, all about the new baby, and when her stories failed her, she read to me from her iPad because she just wanted me to hear her voice (I joked later that it was if she was reading to me as I fell asleep, only hopefully not for the last time). I only wish I'd been more awake, because I'm sure I would have loved to hear her dulcet tones as she read from *Fairy Tale* by Stephen King like it was Dr. Freakin' Seuss (it was what she'd been reading over the holidays and she figured what the hell). I wonder if she paused at lines from *Fairy Tale* like "Sometimes the most horrible things are what give us strength" or "You never know where the trapdoors are in your life, do you?" or

"Fright and loss leave residue" or "The unknown . . . is the scariest thing there is."

Or perhaps she read, "There's always someone at fault, which is not the same as blame."

*   *   *

I would come to understand this about that incident and its aftermath: It was all my fault. I had put all these wonderful people through a living hell. It didn't much matter that I'd been trying to save Alex—what came after was something we'd all have to heal from together.

Though I was mostly in a coma, somewhere deep in my soul I already knew that Kym would have to agonize over dealing with doctors, making decisions about my care, handling the outside world that was already banging on the doors of Renown for information, all the while heartsick at what had happened to her brother with whom she was so close. I knew that my mom would never be able to rid herself of the first sight of my shattered body, my busted eye, of her eldest-born intubated, wired, his breathing horrifying, the lottery numbers of his life flashing as machines beeped and whirred and filled nonexperts with dread and terror, like the fear you feel on an airplane when it's buffered and battered by terrible turbulence, desperately hoping that the flight attendants don't betray on their faces the panic they feel. I knew that Kayla would forever wonder why she heard a helicopter, would giggle at the sight of all that snow, and then would fall face-first into an avalanche of terrible news. I knew that Nicky would always faint, would always be found by her daughter, would always pray she could get a flight to Reno because she thought she had to say goodbye to me. I knew that Dave Kelsey would forever have a dream of a wheat field and a thresher. I knew that Rory Millikin would mourn what happened to me and feel the agonizing congruence of it with what happened to his brother decades before. I knew that I had filled Alex's mind with images he'd never disperse, never fully expunge from a life that was only just gaining steam and purpose. I knew Jesse Corletto would always field the call that said, "We did the best we could." That was such a painful thing for my buddy to swallow, especially as he knew he now had to go down to the hospital, meet my sister, and coach her through whatever was next—and all this without saying anything about the devastating call he'd received. I knew that Rich would forever sound frantic and frustrated on a twenty-minute 911 call; Barb would see the color of her uncle's skin every time she closed her eyes, because it was the color of my skin on the ice.

And I knew that somewhere in Reno, my daughter Ava would sit with her grandmother and be told what had happened to her father.

*　　*　　*

Frank spent hundreds of dollars that day, doing everything he could to distract and entertain Ava and her cousin Bella. Eventually, though, it became clear that someone had to tell Ava what was going on.

Kym had already reached out to Ava's mom, Sonni, to keep her fully in the loop of what was happening. She had told Sonni that Ava was safe, that I'd had an accident, and asked her how she wanted Ava to be told. Because it was becoming clear that I was going to survive the incident at least, a plan was hatched to keep Ava away from seeing me in the hospital—who knows what the sight of my battered body all hooked up to machines might have done to her, though everyone agreed that it would be for certain too much. It was also agreed that my mom would head to the hotel to tell Ava as much as she thought she could handle.

Along with Kym, Nicky, and Kayla, my mom headed to see Ava and to tell her the barest bones of what had happened.

Ava looked stricken.

"Oh no, oh my God. What?" she said. Bella grabbed her in a tight hug.

My family didn't give her too many details, but it was clear that she could see and feel how somber, how serious the adults around her were. Everyone was there, holed up in some random hotel room, all just staring at her. She had to have felt all of that, and I think that's what made her understand the seriousness of it. They tried to be as encouraging as possible—"Daddy's strong, he's going to get better"—but she remained very quiet.

And then, for the next hour, she sat on the hotel bed and watched videos of the two of us over and over and over on her iPad.

It broke everyone's heart. It seemed like she was mourning something, not knowing what her life, my life, would be like moving forward. When she'd awoken that morning, my sweet daughter had been expecting to have me bound back in from clearing a path into an exciting new year, finally freed from the grip of the storm, heading up the mountain and hopefully onto the slopes to ski and snowboard and spend a magical day with her father. Instead, here she was, in a hotel room in Reno, being told that I'd been in an accident, that she couldn't see me, that I would eventually get better . . . And in the face of this unbearable swerve in her life, she'd retreated to videos of us, her silence more heart-shatteringly eloquent than any words she could have said.

It would be another twelve days before I saw Ava.

*   *   *

No one slept much that first night. Everyone lived minute by minute, hour by hour. At some point that day my family and friends had learned that miraculously none of my organs were ruined, my spine was intact, my heart working, and that there probably wasn't any brain damage. Taken together, this information helped it dawn on everyone that I was going to live, and perhaps even recover significantly, if not fully.

It was something like a miracle. And it was underpinned by the love from the community. People brought food to the various hotel rooms that had been organized by the mayor and others; no one could do enough for my family.

That first sleepless night, Kayla lay in bed with Mark, and they discussed how I'd been in the days leading up to the incident.

"His spirit knew what was coming," Kayla said. "It was so tangibly different than the Jeremy we've always known. I think somehow, he *knew*."

As for me, across town at Renown hospital, amid the beeping and clambering of an ICU, my spirit was suspended in a liminal space, at the very edge of life, my bones shattered, my lungs pierced, my eye swollen, my molars cracked. Occasionally I'd slip my toes out from under the blanket, until someone noticed, and they'd re-cover me. They couldn't know—hell, could I have even known?—that this simple act of rebellion was just one more flowering of my recovery. When I'd decided to breathe on the ice, when I'd fought falling unconscious, when I'd looked death in the face and rejected its charms, with each new breath, chiseled as each had been out of the raw air, I'd established a continuum of recovery that could only ever be as a one-way street. To go backward could never be an option. My only job moving forward would be to move forward, to each day get a little farther down the road of reconstruction and healing. So over and over, in the depths of that hospital night, my family elsewhere—unrested and devastated in rented rooms—I slipped a toe out from under the blanket and felt the slight chill of a bland, beige hospital room; a nurse would notice, cover me up; but something in the very depths of me, the man who had faced fears one by one, the boy who had always had a place to land on that proverbial mattress of love, the father-brother-son-uncle-friend, something deep in me pushed my toes back out, over and over and over.

Unknown to me, too, phone calls were being made, recovery plans delineated, surgeries planned. A master surgeon who happens to specialize in reconstructing people with crush injuries (fortunately for me, Reno is the perfect place for his skills, given all the mining and skiing that takes place in this part of Nevada) was already hurrying back from his own winter vacation in Colorado to the hospital, where he would perform miracles with what was left of my rib cage.

Ava knew; my mom knew; my family and friends knew; and then the world knew. Waking on January 2, readers would have found this in *The New York Times*:

The actor Jeremy Renner was in critical but stable condition after being hospitalized with serious injuries from an accident while plowing snow in Nevada, his representative said in a statement.

I would spend six days in the ICU in Reno, then six more in a Los Angeles hospital. And because I only do things I'm good at, pretty quickly I determined that I would be the worst patient ever.

8

FLAIL

My first scheduled surgery was performed on the morning of January 2, 2023.

In the hours after the incident and my admittance to Renown, various doctors had weighed in on what the most pressing needs were for my survival. Fairly quickly it was decided that my chest cavity and my mangled leg were the most important issues to address. My spine seemed unaffected, incredibly; my brain had also escaped any obvious damage. Still there were questions about some of my organs—liver, lungs, diaphragm—and those would be assessed during the forthcoming surgery.

I had multiple broken bones in my face—my orbital socket was cracked, but I'd also fractured my cheekbones in two places—but it was agreed that these fixes could wait. My eye had been duct-taped back in place, and it seemed like my eyesight hadn't been affected (actually, it had—to this day I swear it's better than it was before the incident). This was yet another incredible miracle. On that first day in the ICU, it had been determined that my orbital nerve had somehow avoided being pinched between the broken bones—if that had happened, my eyesight would've been *no bueno*. And the breaks in my face weren't life-threatening—to fix these kinds of broken bones, given how delicate the procedures can be, it's important to get the swelling to reduce first in any case.

There was also the question of *confidence*. The plan for my face changed three times in the first few days, and though everyone's face is important, as an actor it's a huge part of my day job—any surgeries had to be done with my complete buy-in, and would probably be best saved until I could get back to the best city in the world for plastic surgery, which is, duh, Los Angeles.

So those surgeries could wait. Now, though, I faced a major surgery to fix the worst of my injuries. Thank God a superhero was already in the skies heading one thousand miles west to fix me.

*   *   *

Hearing about my injuries, the incredible mayor of Reno, Hillary Schieve, had made a call to the man she knew could help save my life.

The doctor who was flying in from his Colorado vacation, ROC Trauma & Fracture physician Dr. Peter Althausen, is known by the nickname "The Carpenter." Hearing Hillary's plea, he had immediately cut short his vacation and flown back to Reno. When Dr. Althausen studied the 3D images of my chest on his arrival, he would see that twelve ribs were shattered on my right side and two on my left. When a rib breaks in one spot, it's considered a fairly simple fix, but when it breaks in two or more places, then it's much more complicated. Such injuries are called a "flail chest" because the chest cavity no longer has sufficient structure to be useful. This was the case for ten or eleven of the ribs on the right side. And a flail chest is a really difficult thing to fix.

The state of my rib cage, all shattered and skewed bones, was why breathing had been so impossible from the first seconds after the incident. "The Carpenter" told Diane Sawyer in a later interview that the problem had been that when I tried to take a breath, instead of filling the chest cavity with air, because the rib cage no longer had a solid structure, the cavity caved in instead of expanding, causing the flail chest and critical difficulty in breathing. This along with the ruined state of my left leg, which was badly broken (the break was a spiral break, presumably caused by the rotation of the steel tracks as they crushed me), were the things that were top of the list for immediate remediation.

Dr. Althausen was just one more incredible blessing in this whole incident. He simply loves his subject and is world-renowned for it. In fact, he's a self-professed nerd who was reportedly more than happy to travel from Colorado to fix my flail chest. Dr. Althausen had pioneered a procedure to make such a repair. The problem with so many broken ribs was that some of them were broken in multiple places, making reconstruction extremely difficult. But Dr. Althausen, having worked in Reno for years and seen every kind of skiing and mining crush injury, developed a system whereby titanium plates would be used as a basis by which the broken bones could be screwed to the metal. Once you repair a few of them by attaching them to the plates, the other ribs tend to fall into place, meaning you don't have to have the same number of plates for the number of broken bones. The body just naturally bonds to the metal and others follow suit, the chest partially repairing itself. This would mean I'd have a chest cavity filled with titanium, just not as much titanium as you might imagine.

It's a genius technique, and it saved my life.

*   *   *

In addition to the ribs and my leg, during that first major surgery doctors worked to assess my organs. First up was a repair for my liver laceration. Then, the surgeons did a survey of some of my other major organs. They checked whether my diaphragm was also lacerated, as had been feared (turns out it wasn't, which was another huge stroke of luck). Similarly, my lung was also not punctured—another miracle, because punctured lungs greatly increase the chance for bacteria and infection. My liver seemed fine, too.

Having scanned my innards, the surgeons shifted their attention to my broken left tibia and my ankle: just as in my chest, titanium rods were inserted into my leg to fix the shatter, and screws were secured in place to stabilize the gnarly break in my ankle.

There was still a long road to travel, and it would take weeks to discover all the things that were broken in my body—one thing, in particular, would come back to haunt me in the months to come. But for now, I was at least stabilized; the first surgery, though extensive, had been a success, and once again I'd been delivered of numerous miracles.

*   *   *

When I regained the first vestiges of consciousness after my first surgery, I knew what I had to do.

I had been on life support, then had my ribs fixed, my leg, my ankle, then back on life support again—but when I finally started back into conscious life, I saw my family there, all at the foot of the bed, squeezing my toes and talking to me, and I wanted to make a gesture that could begin our shared healing.

I was still intubated, but I wanted to acknowledge, as quickly as I could, what I'd already intuited about what I'd put my family through. I didn't yet even know the full extent of even the half of it; I had been clearing snow, I'd fallen and been crushed, I'd spent forty-five minutes on the ice, I'd been helicoptered out, and, after that, much of my next two days had been spent deep in a haze of heavy sedation. But my family had had no such relief. They'd been very much awake for all of it, massed in a waiting room or in bare hotel rooms, pacing and prognosticating, doing their best to breathe just as I had, trying to support each other, find relief any way they could with such a monumental disaster in their collective hearts.

Much later, I would sit down with everyone and ask them to tell me, minute by minute, what they'd faced that day and in the immediate aftermath (much of this book's reconstruction of those hours when I was in a coma came out of those later sessions where I invited my closest friends and family to share their experiences).

But for now, I was slowly appearing back in the world, the deep sedation slipping out of my bloodstream, for the second time in two days coming back to life. I was cuffed to the rails of the bed (people who are intubated often try to pull the tubes out—I sure would have done so given half a chance), but I asked for one hand to be released.

I brought my hand up to my chest, and to my family around the bed I signed in ASL, "I'm sorry" and "I love you."

I caused this heartache; it was entirely my responsibility. I felt so bad that my actions had caused so much pain.

Then I signaled that I needed a piece of paper. On it, in the scratchiest handwriting you can imagine, I wrote this:

Holy fuck . . . I love you all, I'm so sorry. I love you all so much.

Still filled with narcotics and painkillers, the note might have come out a little garbled—though I happen to think it looks kinda cool and someone should make a T-shirt out of it—but what it lacked in penmanship was made up for in sentiment, which was deep and real and true. I was filled with a sense of both sorrow and joy, sorrow for what I'd done to my family, and joy that all the people I loved in my life were there, at the foot at the bed. Already I could see that the incident could serve as a beacon of love to which we could all give our undivided attention.

I knew if I said I was sorry that they would know what I meant. So when they worked out I'd written "Holy fuck," a peal of laughter filled the room—my family recognized the essential me.

Someone said, "He's back!"

Someone else said, "And he ain't fuckin' around!"

Alex thought, *That's him. He's still there. He's going to be fine. It's just going to be a long road. He's not going to die, thank God. I'll take Jeremy in a wheelchair with one eye and no legs and fucking nubs for fingers. He'd still be the coolest motherfucker.*

The failure to make that leap across the tracks of the snowcat, and everything that accrued from it, might seem a strange thing to focus on as I first regained consciousness, but that failure, and my sorrow for it, became the driving energy of me waking in the first place. I kept thinking, *Damn, I was supposed to take everyone skiing that day. They were all prepared, making breakfast, getting their skis ready. I was supposed to just be clearing the driveway.*

I'm the oldest of seven and have been blessed with a nurturing personality because of my position in the family, so I never want to disappoint them—I always wanted to lead with courage and demonstrate by my actions how to move forward in life, always with integrity and always by amassing information and taking action.

And I just failed; I fucking failed. And I was sorry for that, and sorry for a whole lot of other things. The energy of my sorrow would eventually drive my desire to heal faster than should have been possible, but that wasn't about me, either—it would become the kinetic energy by which the more I healed, the better my friends and family would be so that I wouldn't have to carry so much of this sorrow and I wouldn't have to burden my family with my failure.

I couldn't get over the fact that I had ruined New Year's (because I had) and it would take time to understand the road I was on, the road my family was on. A ruined New Year's would be the least of it.

I had put all that fear and terror onto Alex, who had to hold my arm for forty-five minutes and look at his uncle bleed out on the ice. That poor kid will never be the same because of me; he can't unsee that shit. Neither could any of my family who saw me in the hospital, on life support for three days, a man who could die at any time. My daughter had had to retreat to videos of us, deep in a kind of childlike sorrow for which she had no words, just a sinking feeling in her stomach and a hole the shape of fear in her heart. But my family had been through a lot before that first day of 2023. We've had a bunch of tough losses on my mom's side, from cancer, crib deaths; my grandmother has lost three of her kids already (she's ninety-six!), so there's a toughness that comes with that. But we're not a sky-fallin', Chicken Little family. We have problems to solve, and we solve them.

So even at those earliest moments of waking, I wanted to use the failure as my energy and perspective, as my lodestar. I had to love these people as hard as I could. They were all there for me, they'd murder someone to keep me safe. I have a big, strong, deep love-running family—they're just as gangster for me as I would be for them. (That said, the family has gotten so big on both sides that I don't even know all their names. Sometimes I find myself thinking, *Who the fuck is this one?*) That's why I put my own life on the line for my nephew; I was never going to let that machine crush him! Not happening, not on my watch. I couldn't have lived with that, couldn't have imagined if it was the other way around. I shudder to think . . . I would not be a good man right now—I'd be haunted if anything had happened to Alex that day.

I needed to put those thoughts aside, though. I had to clear my head to focus on recovery, just as I'd focused on breathing.

In the coming weeks and months, I would focus on love and how that love kept getting deeper and deeper across my whole extended family. And I would come to understand how love heals all broken bones, no matter how many.

*   *   *

If I didn't have that family, perhaps I wouldn't have been sorry in the same way, if at all. I was so lucky to have something so precious to live for. Perhaps I would have given up the ghost, would rather have died right there on the ice if I didn't have these wonderful people to survive for.

I owed them my life.

What was notable to me about my initial instincts was that I didn't feel the need to talk about work or my career; all that could wait. Instead,

I focused on my family and on my recovery, to the exclusion of pretty much everything else.

I'd faced the ultimate hardship—and it wasn't my first hardship—but the word "hardship" itself felt strange, because to me, none of it was hard if I focused on what I could do to get back to my family and further my recovery in that moment. The only thing we have control over in our lives is our perception of things, and in this instance, as soon as I got out of the coma, I was determined to fight any feelings of giving up, of letting go.

No, I was going to fight harder than I'd ever fought before, even if it meant I was a challenge to be around. And it's not as if this fight came from a place of being a super-positive guy—in fact, I recently described myself as "kind of a cranky, cynical, grubby cat motherfucker." (I stand by every word of that.) To illustrate just how contrarian I can be, I once had a set of coasters made of phrases I like to repeat: "Please cancel my subscription to your issues"; "If I give you a straw, would you suck the fun out of someone else's day?"; "I'm sorry I called you an asshole. I thought you knew," etc.

Yet, despite this cranky humor, I do believe in the power of a positive thought. This was crucial in setting the tenor for getting better. When it came to my recovery, I had only one route: forward, positive, every day.

That doesn't mean I was an easy person to look after, though. In fact, it made me pretty damn terrible.

*   *   *

I wanted to make some more things clear to my family. I asked for a phone and started to type, as best I could, last words to my family in case this was indeed the end of me.

Here's the first one, a note I wrote to everyone around my bed in that ICU:

> *If I get to a point where I have to live on a machine or serious pain drugs to continue, I choose NOT to continue a dishonest life.*
> *I have lived all I wanted to live.*

I have lived all I dreamed to live.

I have probably overstayed my time on the planet, so it's good that I go anyway.

I have loved all I wanted to love; I have loved more than I ever dreamed to love.

I am honored, overwhelmed, and inspired by all those who reached out in concern, demonstrating love and prayers.

To my family and friends

Your light, happiness, guidance, laughter, and pain have made this moment real enough for me to actually swallow with certainty.

Thank you. For all the love we share. It's immeasurable and immorally abundant dammit!!!

It felt like a victory to be able to write these words. How many of us, when faced with an imminent end, could say that we have lived all we wanted to live, all we dreamed to live; loved all we wanted to love, loved more than we ever dreamed to love?

That's how it felt for me. Something in the dying on the ice, on the fight to make a single breath, then another, then another, something about waking up from surgery, something about already being on the one-way road to survival, to somewhere more wonderful than mere survival, something about all these facets of the last two days filled me with a deeper sense of love than I'd ever had before. If I had to go for good, I genuinely went with a sense of gratitude, and fulfillment, and, yes, love.

This is the trick of life: how to feel those things—love, gratitude, fulfillment—without having to die and resurrect, without having to go through incredible trauma and loss. We shouldn't wait for the edge of the cliff before enjoying the mountainside that brought us there. I had been given the gift of looking at my life from 10,000 feet above the world, from that place of exhilarating peace where all energy flowed together and everything made sense. And the sense it made was this: All I had left was an honest life filled with love, and where I could never again, ever, have a bad day. It just wasn't possible anymore.

That phrase—"I have the blessings of knowing what a bad day really is, and I'll never get to have another one ever again"—was one I'd use many times in the coming months and years. It would become a sort of mantra, a talisman for my recovery. How could anything be worse than the snowcat and the physical torture and forty-five minutes of manual breathing and dying on the ice and putting all those traumatic images in the minds of loved ones and strangers alike? How could I have a bad day once Jesse had been told, "We did the best we could?"—a memory he still cries about to this day? How could I have a bad day knowing my daughter said nothing but instead opened up her iPad to watch us together? How could I have a bad day when I'd reminded Barb of her uncle's passing, not twenty-four hours after his death?

The truth is, I had been perfectly happy to go; in fact, I had left this earth, and it had been so fine, so extraordinary, such a serene excitement. But I also knew that leaving the world bodily would have destroyed a lot of people's lives—especially Ava's. I wouldn't want to be responsible for that, and I think that's where my stubbornness fully kicked in. There was no way I'm going to leave a wake of chaos behind for my daughter and my mother and the rest of my family and friends to navigate. That's the reason I fought so hard to come back. Yes, it was guilt, but more exactly it was about love. The guilt was what I'd put on them, the pain that they'd all had to endure, but the love was the real reason I fought. So yes, I only came back for the people around me; otherwise? I'm outta here. Fuck this planet and fuck paying taxes and fuck this war-torn world! I had been genuinely happy to go, but I'm glad I came back, and I'm moved that others fought so hard for me to return. People fought, acted, prayed, and most of all gave their love.

Did the love keep me alive, or did I stay alive to love? I don't think it matters which comes first—chicken, egg, who cares? What mattered was that I was still here, and blessed to be here at that, and now I'd been given an even greater gift than ever before. Now, I fully understand the depths of the love around me, the love we all share.

And what's more, I now knew that love is eternal. There was nothing anyone had to do to earn it; there was nothing anyone could do to break it. The snowcat had tried its best to break me, and though physically it had done a pretty spectacular job, it couldn't reach the organ that mattered the most. My heart was stronger than ever. And what's more, it now had the opportunity to fortify the hearts of those around me, too.

*   *   *

That day Alex brought me a phone that had a video message on it from Ava—her sweet, innocent voice said, "Hey, Dad, I miss you so much, I hope I can see you soon, and I can't wait to if I can't. I love you so much. I hope you're feeling better. Bye! Love you!"

As the message ended, I closed my eyes and nodded once or twice. This was it; this was the eternal love; this was all a broken man needed to understand that he had one job forever, which was every day to get better so that those around him could heal, too.

But still, the thought of what Ava was going through immediately haunted me. So, to her I wrote the following words, again on someone's phone:

To my daughter,

> *My everything, my only thing, my number one,*
> *You already are the best part of me.*
> *You've become a tremendously inspired woman at such a young age. Your grace, thoughtfulness, and constitution are what makes me so proud. You have so much to love, so much to live, and so much to give. You will be your own teacher now; I'll just be in your heart and mind always guiding . . . Daddy is always with his daughter.*
> *My . . .*
> *Garden of stone*
> *Best part of me*
> *Coming home.*

I can see in that note that I was still unsure I'd make it, at least physically—but I also knew that coming back from death had proved to me that there's an eternity to energy that continues beyond our bodily demise. How much of a comfort this would be to a grieving ten-year-old I didn't want to find out. Yes, she is preternaturally intelligent and sensitive, and our closeness meant that there had been few wasted moments in her ten years. But still, no child should have to face losing a parent so young.

There's been a lot of death in our family, those cancers and crib deaths. But I've always tried hard to not hang on to loss. For me it's important to move through loss to the other side, otherwise you'll sink. Everyone has the right to grieve, but I also believe that when you change the perspective and find the joy in the new reality, your grief can become the signpost to a way forward. Already, in those early days in the ICU, I knew I had to accept the new reality of my body. Who knows, maybe I'd just be a collection of broken bones with my brain in a jar—might that be my new reality? It sure looked that way on the ice. But I would have to work on my perspective, and that of those around me, so that grief didn't make us atrophy.

My job for Ava was to survive and be better for her. The stronger I was, then the stronger she would get. Getting stronger would rid me of the duty of that grief and guilt and regret. The key to all of it is to always propel forward. There's no other way. There's only one direction here, because we all know the alternative, and nobody wants that.

My words to her may have been "Be your own teacher," but the underlying message was this: I would always be with her because my energy is part of the energy of everything, and don't grieve forever. Move forward. Take the next step. Take action. And love with all your heart always.

I hoped she wouldn't have to grieve at all; now, with the first surgery behind me, though I wasn't out of the woods—not even remotely—the first glimmerings of a survival road stretched out before me, like a ribbon of asphalt heading somewhere into a distant sun-blocked horizon.

*   *   *

Alex sat with me regularly in the ICU, and knowing what I'd put him through, it was important that I told him as soon as possible that we had to shape the emotional narrative of the previous day so that we could not only survive it but prosper.

I was still pretty loopy, hopped up on pain meds, yet I was clear with him.

"It's not 'poor me Alex,'" I slurred, "it's 'fuck yeah!' I got to survive and now I get to heal. I'm not dead, I'm not gone. So why are we going to look at all this as some fucking terrible thing? Yeah, it sucks, but are you going to keep looking at it like somebody pissed in your cereal or somebody spit on you or called you a bad name? There's no point in looking at it like that."

Alex knew the stakes were as high as you can imagine. He even said later that because I survived, he got to stay the same person—"I don't know who I'd be if he was gone" were his exact words—and, better yet, in fact everybody gets to be a little bit better versions of themselves because of what we'd all been through.

*   *   *

For a few years after he turned eighteen, Alex headed out on his own, what he calls his "time of Vagabond Inc." He lived for a while on the streets, sometimes in a bus sometimes not, bouncing around from Sacramento to San Francisco to Los Angeles and many points in between. In a large family filled with big characters, Alex had wanted to forge his own path, away from everyone's strong opinions about who and what he should be. He would always be invited to family events, of course, but he seldom showed up, and when he did, he admits now that he didn't love the fact that we all had thoughts about what he should be doing, how he should be living. For a while we didn't see him at all, that is, until everything changed the summer of 2020.

That year my extended family threw our usual Fourth of July celebration, and Alex, now in his mid-twenties, showed up. He arrived with two buddies a couple of days before the holiday, and then hung around. By July fifth the rest of the family had gone, leaving just me and Alex and a few of our friends.

At some point Alex and I found ourselves alone. It had been so long since we'd talked, so long since I'd seen him in person, but I'd been around him my whole life. I felt like it was the right time to give him a Renner Talk. Accordingly, and with judicious use of the double-finger jab into his jugular notch, I spent hours describing who he really was to him, but it wasn't all bad: I told him how much I cared about him, how much he'd clearly grown during his Californian Rumspringa . . . I'm not sure he'd realized how much I'd be paying attention to him, but I really wanted to connect with him and tell him some hard truths, so that's what I did.

From there, things really changed between us. Something in that talk cemented our connection. From then on, I found myself leaning more and more on Alex. To be a full-time actor and to run two properties, one in LA and one in Tahoe, and to have all the vehicles needing upkeep, and the logistics of making sure everything got looked after . . . well, it all left me a bit weary, but Alex had really stepped in to pick up the slack. I ended up turning to him for help on a hundred little things to keep the Tahoe house especially running smoothly. He's especially good with vehicles, and I have a ton of them. A few months after our big July Fourth talk, Alex started working for me, and in some capacity he's been working with me ever since.

But it's more than just logistics—he's told me that it feels like, with our newfound connection and my desire to pressure him to live a more productive life, he's getting a "dad experience" later in life (his own father lived in Sacramento and Alex grew up in Modesto; they were close, but they didn't see each other every day because of the distance). I call him "son" and he'll jokingly call me "Dad." Our relationship is not without its challenges—there are days I don't want to be a father figure to my adult nephew—and I can get pissed off with him. Sometimes Alex can get stuck in a place where he doesn't do anything—I think this comes from depression, and I'm sympathetic to it, but it's also true that it can stanch his ability to *act*, which is something I wish he could overcome. Depression is something he's struggled with his whole life, but these days I think it's happening less and less because the more time we spend together, the more it seems like he's finding his purpose. That's not all down to me and my two fingers in his throat—it's coming out of his own development, his own maturity.

But even though I love him and take care of Alex the best I can, he knows he still has to do life for and by himself. That's true of all of us—we all need to be connected to our own sense of accountability and responsibility. I hold that line with myself, too, and with the people that I surround myself with. The essence of accountability and responsibility is this: If you do the work, it pays off—so just do the work.

It's imperative, too, that we love ourselves and be confident in ourselves. How do we find that confidence? Take one step, then take another step, and then guess what—you're walking! On the ice I knew that I had to breathe out, then breathe in, then breathe out, then breathe in. That's how I knew I was breathing! This is the essence of living a purposeful life, whether you're in extremis, as I was after the incident, or whether it's just some dull-ass Tuesday. We have to be at all times purposeful with the things we do in our lives; otherwise nothing has value.

I already knew that purpose would be my secret weapon when it came to my recovery. And it would start by me taking control of what the world knew about what had happened to me.

9

WORST PATIENT EVER

The biggest—and *only*—mistake my sister Kym made in the days after the incident was to give me back my phone.

Kym had been a godsend. She had handled the press; had disseminated updates on my condition to the wider family; had been integral in making decisions about my treatment, including corralling the various doctors into creating a cogent treatment plan; had kept copious notes and taken many photos and videos to document literally everything that was happening; had talked to my managers and agents and stakeholders in my career every three or four hours and for weeks thereafter to work out what the future looked like for me; and had made sure the situation with Ava was handled with delicacy and love . . . She was a superhero, the rock around which my broken family coalesced, a kind, solid, deep-feeling beacon of humanity when everything had seemed lost.

But yeah, she fucked up once: She gave me back my phone *way* too early.

After the surgery was over and I was awake, it was time to get extubated.

This is not a pleasant process.

I was mostly awake for it. What they do is roll you onto your front and then yank the tubes out, leaving you flopping around on the bed like a fish on a dry dock. The whole thing manages to be both a magical moment—finally you're breathing on your own—mixed with the horror of the actual process of removing the tubes. The image of it is burned into my brain . . . but still, this was an incredible moment of progress.

To celebrate, my incredible sister figured it was safe enough to let me see some of the good wishes and love I'd been receiving via text and video message, so she willingly handed me my phone.

She should have known better.

The news of the accident had leaked by the end of January 1, and the family and my team had put together a press release to get ahead of speculation. In the release they'd tried their best to keep any description of my condition as generic as possible, saying that it was "critical but stable." But no good deed goes unpunished—immediately journalists and keyboard warriors were homing in on the wording, wondering if it was a made-up term, or an obscure medical term that didn't actually make any real sense, and, anyway, what the hell did it mean exactly? Journalists were calling constantly—at one point Kayla looked at her phone and saw a British number and couldn't begin to work out who she knew in London (turns out no one—it was yet another journalist).

But it wasn't the press Kym needed to worry about—it was me. As soon as I got the phone, I brought it up to my face and took a selfie. In the picture my hair is pointing due north, I'm sporting an oxygen cannula, my brutalized left eye looks bruised and heavy behind black reading glasses, but there's the merest hint of a smile on my face, or is it the first glimmerings of triumph in the face of what had happened?

And then I posted the photo on my Instagram. I added a caption:

Thank you all for your kind words🙏
Im too messed up now to type. But I send love to you all.

This was the evening of Tuesday, January 3, only about sixty hours after the incident.

Almost immediately, Sam, my publicist, contacted Kym.

"Are you guys lying and making shit up?" Sam said. "Look at this picture. He looks great. He looks worse in the poster for 'Mayor of Kingstown,' season two."

Sam was not wrong.

(The poster was subsequently changed to make me look less beaten up after the news of the accident broke.)

But there was a serious point to the post. I usually distrust social media, especially sharing anything private, but I felt like it was my duty to share. I know that some people in the public gaze don't show anything, no weakness, no sickness, and that's fine. In this case, I don't think I had a choice because already so much of it was in the public arena. It wasn't like what happened to me happened in private, or in a hospital or something—I was out in the world, there was video footage of the paramedics and the sheriff's department, helicopters were flying over my property. My hand was forced, but I'm glad that it was, because it was the start of me forging an intimate relationship with the public about my recovery. Obviously if no one gave a shit, then I wouldn't have posted anything, but I got the sense early that people genuinely cared, which was so moving to me and truly contributed to my sense that I had to recover for everyone, not just (or even) for me. So in posting that photo I wasn't just correcting the record because my daughter hears stuff in school—"no, I'm not losing my leg, folks, it's fine, don't worry about it, we're all good, and no, I'm not dead!"—but I was also setting the tenor of the ongoing relationship I would have with the wider world, which was that this incident was above all a triumph, a victory of love and perseverance and survival against the odds. So that's the great thing about social media; when you have a big platform, you can not only kill falsehoods but also use that platform to spread a better, happier, more loving message.

And I figured I was walking out of that ICU in a couple days anyway.

Little did I know I was gone, dead to the world, in a coma for days, and on life support.

Silly me.

A dimly lit hospital room. The purring machines pulse with air and chimes like some twisted sound machine.

"Hey . . . *heyyyy* . . . Alex!" I whispered, conspiratorially. "Alex! You hear me?"

"Wha— what is it Uncle Jer?" Alex whispered back.

"You gotta help me break out of here," I said. "It's time!"

In the days after that first surgery, a growing urgency to get out of Reno was building in me.

For a start, another major storm was coming, and the last thing I wanted was for me and my family to be stuck in Nevada any longer than we had to be—especially the family, as they were holed up in various hotels, away from their families, having to deal with doctors and press and movie people and all the trauma they'd been through. I felt like I'd already put them through enough, and now that I was stable, and the life-threatening issues were at bay, the rest—to my mind, at least—was merely picking off each physical problem one at a time while continuing to heal. I didn't want to be in Surgical ICU Room 5S68 any longer than absolutely necessary, which in my mind was day four-ish after the incident. Sure, I'd been wheeled into the ICU on January 1 in the worst state you can imagine; the next day I'd had the major surgery to fix the leg and the chest; January 3 I'd come out of intubation and was breathing on my own (and posting pictures on Instagram), so by January 4? Let's get the fuck out of here!

If that seems impatient, it was, but for a very serious reason. Hospitals are wonderful places for saving lives, but they're less effective as places where people heal, physically and mentally. Not the least of the issues is the fact that they never really leave you alone. Beyond the beeping of the machines and the general hum of a hospital all around you, there was a constant parade of doctors, nurses, lab technicians, X-ray technicians, and orderlies, and I was forever being wheeled down two floors to have yet another set of X-rays taken. Beyond worrying I'd glow in the dark for the rest of my life, I wished there could be greater coordination among all the various medical departments so that they could perhaps do *one* set of X-rays and CAT scans instead of the multiple ones they kept ordering. I realize it didn't help that the snowcat had managed to break or mangle so many disparate parts of my body, but still.

I don't mean to sound ungrateful because I truly am not—I owe my life to every single one of the people who worked at that hospital. On the surface, I was just tired; never being left alone means it's impossible to get a stretch of time where I could get into a deep, restorative sleep. It felt as though as soon as I drifted off, someone came into the room and needed to check something, take me somewhere . . . And beyond the lack of sleep, there was another profound motivation behind my frustration. It served as a barometer by which I recovered. I wanted out because I wanted to show my family that I was already forging ahead, already replacing the terribly traumatic images of January 1 with images that were uplifting, forward-looking, hopeful, healing.

I needed to escape to show everyone that I was ready to get to the real effort of healing, for myself, physically, but mostly for their hearts and minds. And I still needed significant surgeries in Los Angeles on my face; I wanted to get there as soon as possible.

By the fourth afternoon, I'd hatched a plan. Or more exactly, "hatched" a "plan."

"Come on, Alex, pack up my shit, man," I whispered to him when it was just the two of us in my room. "We're leaving, motherfucker. We're out of here. We've got a small window. Got to fix my face, man . . ."

Note that I was still hooked up to multiple machines, and still required a blood transfusion . . . But to me it was imperative that I get out of Reno.

"Okay," Alex said.

This was my second or third attempt at an escape, and it was just as comical as the first two. As Alex once again packed my stuff into a bag, still in a fetching hospital gown, my exposed ass shining in the breeze, and with multiple lines still in my arms, I made what can only be described as the slowest escape in the history of escapes. Think Alcatraz, but if you can't swim.

The first time I tried to escape, I had just about gotten out of the bed before our plan had been rumbled; the second time, not much further; this third time, Alex and I got out of the room at least, but it must have taken a full ten minutes—me shuffling at a snail's pace, trailing machines and wires behind me, on shattered legs and filled with pain meds—by which point news was spreading that Mr. Banana was on the move.

Out in the hallway, a host of nurses, doctors, and other family members, including my mom, were waiting for me.

"We're leaving!" Mr. Banana Thirty-Eight announced.

Someone turned to my mom and said, "He needs a blood transfusion . . . He's not going anywhere."

"Fuck you guys!" I said. "I'm out of here. I want to sleep!"

I looked at the doctors; the doctors looked at my family; my family looked at me. Alex looked at the ground.

And then a nurse sidled up to me and, with more patience than an actual saint, gently ushered me back to bed.

*   *   *

Something had to give—the lack of sleep was killing me.

A decision was made to hire a kind of bodyguard to keep people out of my room so I could finally get some real rest. My brother-in-law Jeff was that bodyguard; he, along with Alex, slept in the room with me, barring entry except for essential checks on my well-being. (It should be noted that Jeff was also there to stop me from escaping.)

The breakouts might have been funny, but they also signaled my essential—and lifesaving—stubbornness. Stubbornness is my life force. I wasn't being a bully—I would never bully anybody, though there were times I was kinda brutal to people. Nurses drawing blood faced my most insistent ire: "You're missing the vein! You're going to draw air, motherfucker! You're going to miss it . . . and that's a miss, that's a swing and a miss!"

Rather, I was bullying myself, chivvying myself along to go as quickly as possible on the road to recovery.

The day I found brooms and mops and buckets and other janitorial effects in my bathroom didn't help, either.

To me, in my fevered, sometimes fentanyl-d state, discovering that stuff made me think no one thought I was going to make it. Did everyone here think I was going to moan and die like everybody else in the ICU? Had I discovered a janitorial service for *aliens*?

"What the fuck?" I yelled at a gaggle of my nurses. "You think I'm not going to make it here? You think you can store your fucking janitor shit in my bathroom? What the fuck? You think everybody else is moaning and dying around me so I'm going to die, too? This place is like a fucking haunted house. ICU?"

And here I went into full Vincent Price voice mode: "More like a horror movie: *I See You . . .*"

I was on one.

But I was also trying to be funny, because dealing with this many injuries, and being so pumped full of medicines, I was desperate to calibrate my sobriety in the ICU. Humor requires timing. Humor requires intelligence. And humor requires an audience, and the ability to *read* that audience. Humor demands a lot of one's consciousness—you have to be really aware, really present, really clued in to be funny. In trying to be funny, in trying to land the gags, I was simply working out just exactly how fucked-up—or not—I was.

If no one laughed, I was in trouble. I was filled with morphine and fentanyl and whatever else. Thank God for all those drugs, but I really wanted to make the nurses laugh, both because it was a way of calibrating my sobriety, and also I realized that being the Worst Patient in the World, they needed some light relief from my constant Great Escape shit.

How well my jokes landed had a direct correlation to my current lucidity.

So, a janitorial service for aliens? Yup, got a smile at least, which equaled an adequate amount of lucidity, though I'm not sure the Vincent Price impersonation quite landed as I'd hoped.

*   *   *

On the fifth morning in Reno, I wrote the following notes on a phone:

> Well, I woke up
>> Moving my legs
>> Goddammit!!!
>> Now this really is my plight
>> My decision
>> I didn't want to wake up with . . .
>> Going [to] ice my legs. While talking with the nurses about [what] my chances to even live are, . . . in the same sentence, I am answering quietly that I'm the only one to determine [that]
>> And now realize that I have to steer this ship of bones to shore with all this love. Dammit

Ship of bones—damn right; that's certainly how it felt by Thursday, January 5. And this ship of bones was clearly torn. Though I would have loved someone to tell me what my long-term prognosis was, the question itself was entirely misguided. The answer lay within me, not externally. Only I could determine the future path of my life. This was always true— why would it be any different after this incident? If we truly believe that we have no control, that the major (and minor) things that happen to us are foisted on us by some exterior force, and that we have no say over the direction our lives take, then what's the point of any of it?

I have never felt that way. I have always forged my own path, however difficult or even impossible it might have seemed. Going through this incident didn't absolve me of my responsibility to myself, however much divine intervention I'd been fortunate to receive. The truth of that intervention, of all the miracles so far, made it even more imperative that I not squander the gifts. I had been bathed in love by so many people that it was now my job to survive, and more, to prosper.

Asking a nurse about my future? As unfair and as understandable as yelling at them for poking at me at three a.m. or storing mops in my bathroom.

*   *   *

While I hope I was more of a tyrant in my own mind than I was in real life, it's probably true that I came across as more charming and witty in my head than was actually apparent to those around me. But when my rant about "I See You" landed, I found my sobriety, and it also served to give a little relief to my family. Being funny like this helped them see a little bit more of my brain function, see that I was lucid enough to be something like the Jeremy they'd always known.

Wanting so desperately to get out of Reno was just another part of my sobriety. It was one of the ways I was able to not focus on my pain, too. And I wasn't trying to make a break for it solely because it sucks being in the hospital. The truth for me was always about trying to find my brain. How do I find my consciousness?

I knew, too, that a storm was coming in and we only had a short window to get the hell out of Reno. And we had already scheduled a surgery for my face in LA (the surgery was slated for January 7, aka my birthday).

In the middle of the night before the dawn of my sixth day, I tried once again to escape, calling my mom and telling her I was flying back to LA stat. My poor family—they were operating on zero sleep and the worst nutrition known to man, vending machine snacks and pizzas. Their bodies, their hearts, were in shock; they were walking around like zombies. But there I was, three o'clock in the morning, calling my mom at her hotel. "We're leaving, Mom!" I announced. "I'm packing up. The plane's ready. We're heading back to LA!"

The plane was not ready; the pilot was still hours away from showing up and checking the weather, there was no clearance by Renown for me to leave, on and on. My family were still working out how to even get me from the hospital to the plane to get me back to Los Angeles.

I was a pain in the ass. But I was also a fighter. And I knew I wasn't going to heal in the hospital. To me, hospitals are where you get your stuff fixed and then you get the hell out. That was my thinking, at least, and I was fighting every damn day to make that happen. For their part, Renown reckoned I still needed two blood transfusions, and there was scant motivation for the hospital to deliver a "busted ass motherfucker," as I described myself, to another hospital too soon—for a start, they had to make sure I was stable enough to travel.

But I knew I wasn't going to lie down and just get pumped full of drugs and wait it out. Because I needed to be ready for the battle. I could see already that I would need every ounce of my intellect and insight to face down pain and setbacks. But these powerful painkillers and sedatives threatened to skin my will.

I had to get out. I had to get out now.

*   *   *

Months before the incident, Rory and I had repurposed an old ambulance and driven it from LA to Reno to donate it to the local fire department. Now, it would have one other use for one day.

Kym had confirmed that the Cedars-Sinai team was in place and ready to receive me, so on Friday, January 6, 2023, with the weather cooperating, at least for now, at seven a.m. the pilot arrived to check that it was indeed clear enough to fly me to Los Angeles. Though Renown had been reluctant to have me leave, they also recognized that I was probably not going to take no for an answer, and they cleared me to travel. The fixed-wing JSX private airplane was ICU equipped; all I had to do now was get from the hospital to the airport, three miles south.

That Friday, January 6, the same ambulance we'd repurposed and donated showed up at the loading dock of Renown, and together with a bunch of local firefighters and Alex, I was once again loaded into the back of an ambulance to take the ten-minute ride to Reno-Tahoe International Airport. I never thought I'd be a passenger in my own ambulance, but there I was, on another searingly beautiful day, just like January 1 had been. Then, before I could quite believe it, we were taxiing before our 11:35 a.m. flight south.

And then suddenly we were airborne, flying up into the sharp and bright and clear Nevada air.

I had been in the Reno ICU for six days. As I'd left that day, the nurses had all seemed moved—they were more used to folks never leaving the ICU than this stubborn guy finally making good on his promise to escape (and did I see a hint of relief in some of the eyes that they could put the mops and brooms back in the bathroom?). At some point in the future, I'd come back and thank them and apologize for truly being the worst patient ever.

But for now, a new future beckoned. After more surgeries (and yet more cantankerous behavior at Cedars), I'd finally head home. I was desperate to start my real healing; I was desperate to see my daughter; I was desperate to prove to my family that we could get past this, and, more importantly, that we could double down on the bonds we had by healing together, by celebrating how this chance moment of disaster had forged new pathways of love for us.

It took an hour to fly to Burbank Airport. There, I was gently transferred to another ambulance, to make the twelve-mile drive south to Cedars-Sinai Medical Center. From my prone position in the ambulance, I could only see the blue Los Angeles sky, and as we crested Cahuenga Pass and turned west for Cedars, that Southern Californian sky shone like never before in the high January light.

The next day I would turn fifty-two years old.

Fifty-two, yes, but also, I was a newborn: I'd faced down death on the ice less than a week earlier, and now, even though I would spend another six days in hospital, a kind of faint light was growing in the distant window that was my recovery. Every day going forward had the chance to be as glorious as the undimmed sun of Southern California; it wouldn't be easy, but it would be inevitable: I would get better, I would walk, I would work, I would bring a report back from the edge of death, and that report would make us Renners see our way forward better every day.

*   *   *

But before I could get back to my house in the Hollywood Hills, I faced another set of surgeries and six days at Cedars. I was done with hospitals pretty much the day I woke up, so my attitude in this second hospital wasn't much better now that I was less than five miles south of my house—the tantalizing yet still-out-of-reach home I yearned for in some ways made things worse at Cedars than they had been in Reno.

At Cedars I was once again under the care of multiple doctors—one for blood because I would need two transfusions, another for my face, one for my other bones, on and on. And once again, because of the various and sometimes competing needs of all the medical staff, it felt like no one was talking to each other, which only added to my frustration. It seemed that everyone and his mother wanted X-rays, or CAT scans, or MRIs; everyone wanted blood; someone else wanted this, someone else wanted that. It was bleeding me dry; my arms were like pin cushions—I looked like a junkie. And once again, I wasn't sleeping, which made me a cranky you know what.

Hospitals are not great places if you want to be left alone, and damn I just was not being left alone. The Worst Patient Ever found himself saying things like, "Stop fucking touching me. Stop poking me!"

It didn't help that it was my birthday on Saturday, though I was so pleased to get so many great messages. In Reno Anthony Mackie had flown in from Vegas to see me—Rory brought him by, and when I'd looked up and recognized him through all of the meds and pain, I just found myself in my head apologizing to him as I had to my family. (I had a whole conversation with Anthony in my head—I was intubated at the time—and from his part, it must have been like just watching me die. It was surreal to watch people come say goodbye to me as though I was in an open casket. And yet I also felt so loved because of it; I was a sponge for that love, and it helped me start to heal.)

Rory had once told me that his brother, John, had been that way when he had gotten paralyzed. He had never made it about himself, even though his life had changed utterly in an instant. John had subsequently had a huge recovery, moving from a quadriplegic to a hemiparetic (that is, with one-sided paralysis only) and I had come back from the dead. I like to think that looking outward instead of inward, as John had done, was one of the keys to recovery.

More friends flooded my inbox. As I moved back to LA, my dear pals Sam Rockwell and Colin Farrell recorded a video message for me, singing me happy birthday; Jimmy Kimmel sent a video message, too, which was hilarious; and other friends like Paul Rudd would come by to lie next to me in my Cedars hospital bed. Rudd even made a fake cameo message, pretending as though I were some kind of stranger. "Hey Gerry," he said, "I hear you're a little banged up—got in a fight with a snowblower, apparently? Anyway, I just wanted to send this video, it's really from the heart, I hope you're feeling better, sounds like you are—apparently, you're a pretty tough guy. So maybe I'll get to meet you one day, and wouldn't that be something? In the meantime, take care, and take it easy for a while! And maybe next time just let the snow melt! Feel better, Gerry!"

What I found, too, was that seeing the reaction of my friends convinced me that something really bad had happened to me, that I was truly messed up; you could see it on their faces, which brought home to me the severity of what they were seeing (and also caused me to joke that they were terrible actors who couldn't keep the shock off their faces!). Up to that point I still sometimes tried to tell myself that it was all just a few bruises and scrapes, maybe a cramp or two, that I'd be fine in a few days . . . seeing their reactions cured me of that delusion.

I was to find that with all my deep friendships, everything just got deeper, better. I think that's because we had all been tested in our own ways by the incident and its aftermath. The friends who came to lie in my hospital bed with me, including Rudd, just wanted to nurture me and love on me, and I got that from so many people in the next weeks and months. Friends would try to make me laugh; I ended up making them laugh right back, and all this laughter, and love, opened up a doorway for a deeper sense of ourselves, a deeper sense of friendships.

I'm certain that the deepening of our connections echoed out, like ripples in a lake, affecting their friendships with other people, too. Rudd, for example, was in my hospital bed a couple of times, and the times we shared and laughed and talked and grieved together? I guarantee that shifted his relationships with his own children, with his friends, with everyone. The people I was closest to had looked into something like an abyss with me, and in doing so they had garnered a new, deeper, more connected center to their relationships.

For me, there were times I felt like I was alive during my own wake—I was in a casket but alive, watching everybody act as if I was dead. It could be overwhelming, unnerving.

I had overcome something; I wasn't even sure what just yet. But that capacity to overcome had outperformed even what I hoped it could achieve. I had been tested well beyond my limits, but how do you really know until you are tested what you can get through? How lucky am I to have gone beyond what I had previously thought capable of, and had not only survived, but had already begun to chart the blessings in it? It bore repeating, and I said it to anyone who came by, any friend who needed to hear it: I was going to live the rest of my days without having a bad one. I don't care how fucked-up my knees get. If I get hit by a car or lose some limbs, who cares? That's *nothing*; that's a Monday afternoon! I had been through an extraordinary test—emotional, spiritual, physical, existential—and as I lay in the bed at Cedars, when the thought crossed my mind that maybe I couldn't work again, in the next breath I'd think, "Who cares? I'm just happy to be alive again. Time to take the next step."

*   *   *

But first I faced more surgeries.

On January 7—my actual birthday—the broken bones in my right ankle were fixed and two screws inserted so I could bear weight on that leg (I'd wear a walking boot for weeks). My right knee was very painful, but nothing definitive showed up on the X-ray, so it was decided I'd have an MRI on it sometime later.

And then there was my face. The damage was extensive: I had one floating face bone near my eye socket, a floating pallet, and a jawbone broken in three places. (One piece of good news: An ophthalmologist checked my left eye, the one that had popped out onto the ice, and had found no lasting injuries.)

To repair my face fractures, the doctors went up inside my mouth and inserted plates in my cheek. For my jaw they inserted screws right into the bone of my skull and two more into my lower jaw, to which they then attached rubber bands to create tension, all in order to get everything back into place. I would face six weeks of liquids and soft foods while it all healed (and when I tell you how they got the screws out of my jaw . . . we'll get to that. You might want to take a stiff drink beforehand). I also got an epidural to address the pain in my recovering chest—this made my legs numb for few days, and I had a continual drip of OxyContin to address the pain in my right foot and my face.

But by the evening of my birthday, I'd been moved from the ICU to a regular bed on the eighth floor of Cedars, which was incredible progress given that the incident had been just one week earlier. Still, even this milestone didn't free me from my frustrations. I wanted to get out of Cedars almost immediately. Lying around "healing" was not, as ever, working for me. Even when I wanted to go to the bathroom, I would have to wait for someone to show up to help me.

There was a particularly embarrassing moment after the birthday surgeries, when nature called, and I alerted the nursing station for help. When they didn't arrive instantly—and I mean *instantly*, as they were supposed to have read my mind already—I decided to not wait at all.

Having missed our flight to Lake Tahoe, Ava, Alex, the two pups, and I set out to beat the "storm" on an eight-hour drive north.

I always knew that whatever happened in life, I had a mattress of love to fall on—at Camp Renner with the extended Renner family.

The storm was generational, burying our house in many feet of snow.

The PistenBully is invaluable in mountain areas—without it, we'd be going nowhere. Love it or hate, this is the actual machine that I was underneath.

Just after dawn, New Year's Day, 2023. A few minutes later, everything would change.

There are six sets of wheels on this PistenBully, each helping exert the 14,000 pounds of downward pressure through the steel teardrop blades.

I am intubated. There are one, two, three, four, five, six machines attached to me, belching out ever-changing numbers constantly: the lottery of my new existence, 125, 50, 95, 88/54, 98 . . .

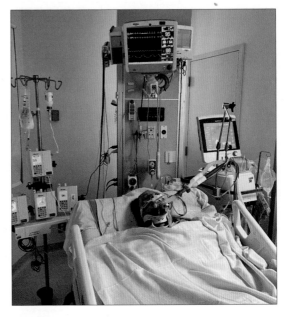

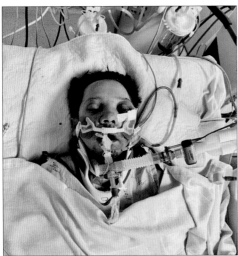

This is what my family walks into at the Renown ICU. Life most definitely in the balance.

(BELOW LEFT) My mom seldom left my side, and often read to me from her iPad . . . including passages from *Fairy Tale* by Stephen King.

(BELOW RIGHT) I would come to understand how love heals all broken bones, no matter how many.

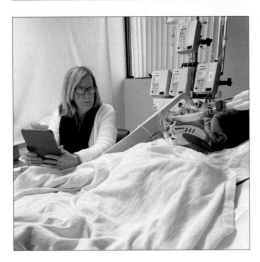

January 3, 2023, two days after the incident—I get my phone back, and this is the photo I post on Instagram. Thought I looked cute (might delete later) ;)

From left: my mom, Rory, Kayla, Jack Millikin, Frank, Alex, and Kym.

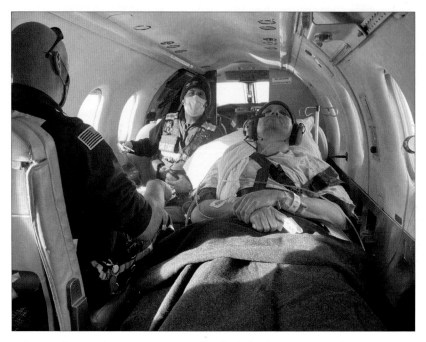

After six days in the Reno ICU, I took a flight back to Los Angeles to continue my recovery.

When my daughter arrived home to see me for the first time since the incident, we fell into each other, quietly sobbing. I asked her to "wait for me," and she did.

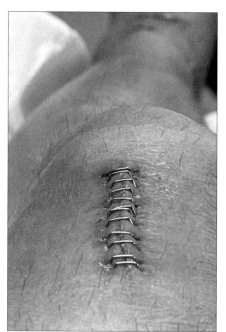
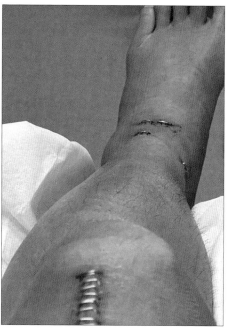

A small reminder that I was now filled with love and titanium.

When it came to rehabilitation, it was imperative I stretch, move, flex, exercise, and create blood flow every day if I was to ever walk again. The "Agreement" was birthed here.

A moment of quiet daddy-daughter time before the storm and before anyone else arrived that New Year's Eve holiday.

I looked at my mom. She'd been with me constantly, usually quietly reading a book and keeping me company.

"Fuck it," I said, "I can do this."

"Jer, you *just* called them!" she said.

"I feel like I've done this routine enough times to do it on my own, Ma," I said.

Yes, I was still on shattered legs, but I had finished the last of my surgeries, my life force was strong, and the bathroom is meant to be a private experience after all. The second I hung up the phone off I went, dragging all the machines behind me, walking on legs that shouldn't be being walked on, conveniently forgetting (or not caring more like) that I am still attached to an epidural, IVs, oxygen tubes, painkillers (obviously working brilliantly), and two clear plastic briefcases that contained blood and goop purged from my healing lungs.

Meanwhile, my mom was frantically calling the desk.

"Get in here!" she said. "He's up! He's dragging his walker . . . into the bathroom . . . and I can't stop him!"

But before she could get any assistance, my poor mom could only stare as I slowly lurched, like the walking dead, and disappeared around a corner with the machines in tow. Then, she watched as the walker was violently discarded from the bathroom like in a cartoon, all the way back into the room of tangled wires and a symphony of screeching alarms.

"Ya see?" I muttered. "I can do this!"

*   *   *

My stay at Cedars was one of the toughest parts of my early recovery.

Even with the chest tubes removed and a chest epidural in place, pain management was a struggle. And though I wasn't eating very much, all the meds still left me constipated, too, which added to my discomfort. I was regularly trying to get to the restroom with a walker (and with the nurses this time), though given how jammed up I was, there was never a need to rush, sadly. But with the ongoing struggle against the pain that seemed to be emanating from every corner of my body, together with the continuing lack of sleep, my moods were fluctuating all over the place. By the end of January 8, I had developed a fever of 102, too.

Notes Kym took around that time are eloquent about the short-term issues I faced and my priorities for recovery.

Wants to be home to heal whenever possible.
Needs sleep assistance.
Rehab to be at home as soon as possible. No rehab facility if possible.
Hates needles and blood draws.

All of this was very true—mostly, I wanted to get out of Cedars, of *any* hospital, and begin the real healing away from beige walls and being woken every twenty minutes. And I truly didn't want to go to a rehab facility because I knew myself, knew my fighting spirit would urge me on without the need of a formal structure. Sure, some people greatly benefit from being urged to do one more rep on a machine, but that was never me—no one ever had to make me do a single extra element of my recovery. As I've said, I knew from the second I woke up (and perhaps even before that) that to get back to a life I recognized, a life where I could be a paradigm for those around me, a life where I was fully present physically and emotionally for Ava and for my family and friends, I would have to push myself every minute of every day to recover, and thrive. No one would ever have to tell me to work a little harder.

When you can see what an end result is—and I had a vivid clarity about where I was heading once I got out of the hospital—then for me, at least, a kind of single-mindedness, some might say bloody-mindedness, kicks in. I had one job for the rest of my life, which was to get better than I was the day before. That's all that mattered. And it wasn't as if I was setting a particularly high bar—to just feel a little better today than yesterday, and better again tomorrow, wasn't scaling Everest or diving to the bottom of the Marianas Trench. Each increment of improvement defined the day's success—could I walk one step unaided, then two, then three, then four? In a couple of weeks could I walk the length of my living room? I don't think many people, including my doctors, gave me any hope of walking normally, and certainly not running again, but then, it would have been unfair of me to expect relative strangers to know what I was capable of.

I knew I'd run again. I knew I'd do everything I used to do, because what is the alternative?

*　　*　　*

I'd long been known for doing my own stunts in movies. I'd learned the importance of that from Tom Cruise.

In my career I've probably done 95 percent of my own stunts—there are a few where it's a distant shot so it doesn't need to be me, but Tom is the guy who taught me how to approach the physical part of moviemaking. I was already an athlete when we first started working together, but on *Mission: Impossible* Tom showed me that you have to treat the job as though you're a *professional* athlete, properly stretching in between takes, making sure you engage a physical therapist, getting taped up . . . You're not just some actor anymore: You're going to the Super Bowl.

But it doesn't always go to plan. During the making of *The Hurt Locker* I'd tripped down a flight of stairs and almost dropped a "dead" body I was carrying, and we'd had to stop production for a couple of days. In Dubai with Tom on *Mission: Impossible—Ghost Protocol*, we'd been at the top of the Burj Khalifa, the tallest building in the world, and I was supposed to be holding on to Tom's leg from just inside the structure while he dangled outside. Tom had a couple of wires holding him, and a harness, but me? I was being held on a rope, and I was wearing slippery slacks . . . and when I looked back, I realized the guy holding me was on his phone.

"Dude," I said, "this shit just doesn't feel very safe. Can you at least get off your phone?"

I'm happy to say I didn't barf on Tom, but it was a close-run thing.

Now, in Cedars, I had to believe I could get back to this kind of physical ability, or something like it. This was a man who had eaten donut holes because that was all he could afford. This was a latchkey kid who, despite there being a key around his neck, always knew there was a mattress of love onto which he could fall. As an exercise in personal growth, I had made a list of my fears and faced them one by one, but a week earlier I had come up against a fear no one could ever have written down on a piece of paper. No amount of imagination could have conjured up what happened to me on the ice; no screenwriter could have created that scene in all its horror. The incident was a fluke of bad luck, bad weather, bad decisions, and yet it also came from the deepest wellspring of love, a love I carried with me every day. I couldn't let anything happen to Alex; this was not a thought-out reaction, but something that came from my very quick, an entirely instinctual reaction to a clear and present danger. The motivation for my character in that moment was clear: It was love. So how could I hope to explain to the otherwise deeply committed staff of a rehab facility that when they thought I was done for the day I was probably just getting started because the fuel for my bones and for my muscles was something both intangible and as real as the new blood that flowed through me? It was love, the kind that moves mountains.

*   *   *

It was clear to everyone that I would be leaving Cedars probably sooner than anyone had hoped or anticipated—no one really wanted to see more walkers come flying out of bathrooms. Accordingly, a family care meeting was called for January 10, where basics were discussed back and forth, like which leg could bear weight (right, not left) and what medications I'd be on after my discharge.

Initially it was expected I'd be going home the following weekend, or maybe Monday, January 16; on January 11 I received a full head-to-toe assessment of my injuries; that same day, there was a call with my preferred rehab guy, Dr. Christopher Vincent. I'd worked with Christopher regularly since 2011, and I knew he was a guy who could match my urgency when it came to pushing myself every day. We agreed to install as much rehab equipment as possible in my house in the Hollywood Hills; along with a whole slew of supplements, we would use balls and bands, rollers, an anti-gravity treadmill, Normatec compression sleeves, you name it—we'd even eventually get a Boost Treadmill, which would help me relearn to walk without the need of putting all my weight on my legs and ankles.

By January 12 we were meeting with a Cedars social worker to discuss the implications of my leaving sooner rather than later. My house was not set up to be effective as a stand-in for a hospital, so we'd need things like a shower chair and a walker and a wheelchair. An electric bed would be crucial, too.

Then there were the issues of home health. Though Christopher Vincent could organize a team for rehab, I'd still require nursing support—I couldn't expect my family and friends to do everything all the time. There were so many things to think about: I would need food plans, specifically meals that emphasized anti-inflammatory effects, given that my entire body was healing and inflammation caused intense, twenty-four-hour pain. We'd need a walkie-talkie so that I could communicate with everyone; we'd need a vehicle big enough and comfortable enough for me to get to doctor's appointments. There would be endless appointments to be managed; I would especially need a pain management doctor. We would have to keep a close tab on visitors; though I was touched that so many people wanted to come by, for the time being my home was a surrogate hospital / rehab center / healing center, and it would be important to limit face time to family and close people in my circle. (Jeff, who had been my pseudo bodyguard in Reno, keeping people out of my room so I could sleep, once again stepped up as pseudo police officer. He created and maintained a Google doc so that everyone could sign up for visits.) And, I was going to tire very easily, and I was going to be in a lot of pain. I'd be migrating from intravenous medications to oral, and there would be a natural diminution in their effectiveness.

None of us quite knew what to expect.

There was so much else. I'd need sponge baths daily and regular movement in bed so that I didn't get bedsores. Do we need a ramp for me to get in and out of the house? How would I communicate with a jaw that was wired in place?

And then there was my right knee. It remained very swollen and very painful. It was clear I needed an MRI, yet given how much my body hurt, I genuinely couldn't say if the pain from that knee was worse than anything else. Was it just twisted badly? Had I busted an ACL (anterior cruciate ligament) or an MCL (medial collateral ligament)? Or was it worse even than that?

On Thursday, January 12, I had another blood transfusion. I lost a lot of blood from the gash in my head, and it takes three months before blood from a transfusion is made your own—after such a traumatic set of injuries, hemoglobin levels are very low, which means the blood you *do* have lacks the healing properties of a healthy person, slowing recovery significantly, hence the need for this second transfusion.

Still, remember how I said it looked like I'd go home on the weekend or Monday the sixteenth?

Friday, January 13—yes, Friday the Thirteenth—I was discharged from Cedars-Sinai Medical Center. I had been obliterated by a 14,000-pound machine, broken thirty-eight bones, and had my eye busted out of my head, had died—had actually died—and then had relearned to breath manually for forty-five minutes. Then, hypothermic and with a heart rate below what should be survivable, I'd been flown in a helicopter to a hospital, had surgeries, had posted a picture of myself on Instagram, then been flown to another hospital, had multiple further surgeries, had thrown a walker out of a bathroom, had two blood transfusions, been nominated and won in a landslide the position of "Worst Patient Ever" in both facilities, and had signed that I was sorry to my beautiful family.

In all, I had spent twelve days in the hospital.

I haven't spent a single night in a hospital since.

PART THREE

RECOVERY

10

WAIT FOR ME

Recovery is a one-way, unpaved road, and despite the love and care of my family and friends, I was still setting off along it alone, not sure of where it would lead.

But I brought to that journey a whole set of beliefs that I'd developed and nurtured over my five decades on this planet.

For a start, I already knew that obstacles, problems, and failures were my allies, not my enemies. Setbacks, far from stanching my ability to move forward, are actually the foundation upon which my successes are built. This is not simply a case of "what doesn't kill you makes you stronger." I welcome obstacles. They give me the fire to burn away everything that could potentially get in my way.

What I am truly afraid of are complacency and comfort. Our span of time on earth is so fleeting, why would we ever be complacent? What are we waiting for? If we're waiting for things to come easy, then it'll be a long wait. Should I have just waited on the ice for the EMTs to arrive? It never crossed my mind, which is good, because if I had waited, they would have had nothing to do when they drove up the Mount Rose Highway. They would have found a half-frozen, empty shell, someone who'd let down everyone he loved.

There was no way that was going to happen.

In life, just as in recovery, all things of value come at a price, be it through suffering and struggle, through surviving hardships, or via the punishing march of time. Time is undeniable; none of us can slow it, stanch it, hold it back. Given that fundamental truth, what the hell are we waiting for?

From the day I arrived back in my house in the Hollywood Hills, with the boxes of fitness equipment still being unpacked, with my bedroom now filled with a motorized bed, I could see that time wasn't going to wait for me: I had to rise to meet it, face it down, work every single second to get back to something called normal.

The first thing I did? I headed straight for my bar and poured myself a glass of red wine.

*   *   *

It was no secret that my medical team at Cedars wanted to keep me in the hospital longer than I wanted to stay. This came back to haunt all of us the first night home; to everyone except me, it felt like I'd left the hospital way too soon.

When I'd been wheeled into my house on Friday, the thirteenth of January, the first thing I saw, dead ahead of me, was my bar. That little bar, up against the windows that look out over my patio and gardens, is the place I find myself most often hanging out—it's comfortable, relaxed, a control center for the whole house. From there I can see outward across the property to my recording studio, but also inward to the sitting room, to my piano, and I can hear everything that's going on in my kitchen from my vantage point at the end of the bar, too. It's always been my favorite spot; I like to prop myself on a stool and let the world come to me.

Getting home that day, the bar represented normalcy, a return to a life I'd been living just a couple of weeks earlier. And that's why I headed straight to it.

As my wheelchair reached the bar, I stood up out of it, still on shattered legs, and poured myself a huge glass of wine.

Now, please understand that I had no medical clearance to actually drink the vino. But I was done with hospitals and limitations. In pouring myself that drink, I was just trying to reestablish something close to normalcy; I wanted to get back into life as soon as possible. I had been through hell, and here, in the bar and with the wine in my shattered hand, I found a tiny glimpse of normal. I was so happy to be home—it was like Christmas morning (even though it was at night). This home had been the focus point of so many great memories, and the bar, especially, had served as the fulcrum of so many of those wonderful times. I'd had so much fun with people there, so much joy, including trying to convince Rory Millikin that I was an actor right where I now stood. This was the first moment in nearly two weeks that I was not in a hospital getting tubed and rolled over and fingered, and I was determined to soak it in.

So yeah, I poured myself a massive glass of Pinot.

Alex saw me do it and freaked out.

"Dude?" he said. "What the fuck are you doing? You can't drink that . . ."

"Alex," I said, "you're going to have to get the fuck out of here. I'm fine." Then there was a pause as I stared at myself in the reflection of the window, not recognizing myself, standing there with a kung fu grip on this proverbial Johnny Depp "Mega Pint."

"I don't know what I'm doing," I said.

Alex knew exactly which meds I was on, and how they would potentially react to alcohol, so he wasn't wrong that I shouldn't actually touch the stuff. But I didn't want to be on meds any longer; I wanted my normal, sane, lucid life back.

"I'm not fucking taking pills," I said. "I won't take that shit."

"You have to," Alex said.

Having that drink in my hand made me feel alive again, even though deep down I knew I was just kidding myself. To recap, I'd gotten home to my house just twelve days after the incident; everything was pinned, my body titanium-filled, contusions and staples and bones still shattered all over my body. But this urge for normalcy, for pushing the boundaries, was what had always gotten me through any trial in my life, not just after the incident. I'd always taken a deep breath, focused on the information at hand, and acted (in all senses of the word). Of course, I was ignoring some key information that night, including the potentially ruinous interaction between pain meds and Pinot. But that urge to struggle and overcome, that ability to fight, that commitment to beating the odds has always been what got me through, and I wasn't about to settle now.

There's one word for all this: hope. Hope is what everyone needs to exist in a state of joy and forward motion. If you don't have hope, you're going to die or kill yourself. To keep imagination alive, however weakly, is the essence of living a happy and fulfilled life.

I have hope. Whether it's committing to breathing even in the depths of the worst pain imaginable or trying to break out of those handcuffs to make the slowest escape possible from a hospital, or even pouring a glass of wine as I walk through my door—or a million other things I clung to in those twelve days—all of it was in the service of hope.

Sometimes hope came right against suffering, though. I did need medication to get me through, I knew that. My brain says, "Hope, hope, hope," but sometimes my body says, "You're a hot mess, motherfucker." To which my brain replies, "Fuck you. I'm a superhero. Let's party." Body replies, "No, motherfucker, we can't even walk yet."

That night a duality in my situation was established—hope, reality, hope, reality—and it has defined my existence to this day as I write this book. In the beginning I could barely run, and it's still difficult, but one day I know I'm going to run a 4.5-second 40 meters. That's just how my mind works. A barrier looks like an opportunity to push through something, not a stop sign.

And I promise this: I'll get there. You will see a fifty-five-year-old man running a 4.5 40 on titanium-filled legs and ankles. Mark my words. My body's going to follow my brain, not the other way round.

Mark my words.

(By the way, when I wasn't looking, Alex scrunched up a piece of paper and dropped it into my wine to make it undrinkable.)

*   *   *

That hope-filled glass of wine was as good as my first night got; in fact, my return home was incredibly challenging.

The key problem was medication. The epidural was removed, and the transition from intravenous meds to oral meds went as badly as we feared it might. I would learn the hard way that night that though I wanted nothing to do with heavy pain meds, keeping ahead of the pain would be crucial, at least in the short term. My body was in shock. When meds go via your gut to your bloodstream rather than directly in, inevitably there's a delay in their effectiveness—think about how long it takes for a headache to respond to a couple of Advil. Best-case scenario, it's half an hour, right? I was on something stronger than regular Advil, but multiply the slowness of oral meds by thirty-eight broken bones and you can get a sense of how badly that first night went.

It was agonizing. At some point in the small hours my mom, who stayed with me all night, figured she needed to get me back to Cedars.

"You were in so much pain," she said later. "I've never seen anyone in so much pain. I was going to call the ambulance to take you back . . ."

Mom and I wept that night; it was agonizing. Mom ended up texting Kym and they decided to call my pain manager, who upped the frequency of my OxyContin, but a painful lesson (literally and metaphorically) had been learned: I couldn't afford to get behind on my pain management.

That is, until a few weeks later, when I went cold turkey.

*   *   *

I had been home for just one day, and through the pain and the struggle and the tears—and in my intense focus on choosing hope—I'd temporarily been distracted from all the normal things in my life. My parental responsibilities, for example, had been pushed to the side. I hadn't wanted Ava to see me in the ICU; I hadn't looked in a mirror for weeks, and didn't want her to see me like that. I was just not emotionally prepared to see her, or to deal with the ramifications if I failed to survive and recover. In my focus on recovery, everything had gotten stripped away, including a lot of good stuff, like being Ava's dad. I hadn't been making her school lunches or driving her places; temporarily, I hadn't been her parent.

In some ways, this was a worse feeling than the incident itself.

Since I'd written her that goodbye note in the first ICU, I'd been so in and out of things, so focused on each minute of recovery and fight, and in so much pain, that my usual state of heart—yearning for and missing my daughter every second that I didn't see her—had taken a back seat. That's how overloaded my mind and body and spirit were.

My usual mantra when returning to LA after work or travel was to ask, "Where's Ava? Get her here now. I can't wait to see her!" But now, I found myself lying on the couch, flatlined, out of it, pain-fractured. It was brutal.

When the door opened that second day and my daughter ran in to see me, it first registered as a concussed surprise, but I immediately forgot what I'd forgotten—she came running to me on the couch and we fell into each other, sobbing. She was clearly scared by what she saw, but we just spent the next few minutes hugging (well, I was able to bring her to me gently with one arm at least) and crying and saying how much we loved each other.

This was the pain and love that I'd lost sight of, and yet always knew I had it to fall back on and motivate me. Her showing up snapped me back into being a father. Yet my usual role as a father—tossing her around playfully, picking her up for cuddles, all the physical stuff we did together—none of that was possible just then, and she could see that, and I could see her see it. Once again in my mind I was still capable of doing all of it for my daughter, but my body could not be her safety net, not yet. When she gets hurt, I take care of her; I'm her protector; but not today, not yet.

She'd seen me hurt before—when she was much younger, I'd broken both my arms doing a stunt on my first day of shooting the movie *Tag*—but this was different level, obviously. I knew I had to face my own limitations honestly for her, so that the two of us could start out on a road of recovery together.

"It's going to be fine," I said, "but I need you to be a big girl and look after me a little bit. I might need something, and if I do, can you be my legs and go get it for me?"

This seemed to delight her, but I could still sense she was wary of how much damage my body had endured.

"Here's what's happened," I said. "Ava, it's just bones, honey. That's all it is. I know I look a little messed up but don't forget it's just bones. Do you remember when your friend Dylan broke her arm, and you signed her big red cast?"

"Yes, Daddy," she said.

"Well, does Dylan still have the cast on?"

"No, it's been off for ages . . ."

"Right, and what is Dylan up to now? Can she do a cartwheel?"

I knew Dylan could do a cartwheel because I'd recently seen her do one.

"So that's one bone she broke, Ava. Dad just has thirty-eight of them. They're all over my body, though, so they can't put me in a cast because I'd look like a mummy."

Ava thought this was funny, and it seemed to calm her.

I was so relieved to feel like a parent again.

I didn't want my daughter to have to learn some hard lessons at ten years old, but at the same time, I knew the coming months of recovery could be gold for her, for us, for everyone around us. She already had a strong sense of self and an amazing presence—everyone remarked on it—but now it was going to get cemented in her forever. What had happened to me was now burned in her soul, and rather than being a wound, it had the chance to be an awesome example of lemonade out of lemons if I was able to outpace what people expected of my recovery. What she went through hadn't been fun or pleasant, but it would serve to loan her incredible information about what human beings are capable of, what life can be if you change the narrative, if you just push through. Those thirty-eight bones were going to heal, and I was going to get better every day, stronger every day, and she was going to witness it.

"You'll see," I said, "but you just have to wait for me. If you wait for me, you'll see. I promise."

"I'll wait," she said. "I promise."

*   *   *

That conversation with Ava, on my second night home, acted as my motivation for everything that came after. If I had been unsure before then, what I was being called to do was now 100 percent clear in my head. Ava was my life force before the accident, but now she was to become my recovery force, my fuel. I would be afforded the privilege to show this girl what I was capable of and inadvertently what she was capable of, too, and I wasn't going to fail.

I couldn't afford to disappoint her any more than I already had. I saw the fear in her face, and that's the last time I would make her scared. I vowed to do everything I could to prevent her from being fearful. In recovering faster than any human had the right to, I would make her confident, strong; I would help her to overcome her fears, and more, to understand what fears really are. In fighting every day to hit milestones, I would give her all these tools she needed to deal with fear.

Being the cause of the fear hurt, weighed heavy on me. Now I had one job, which was to be the guy who rids her of the fear, drives it away. I had to get better so my daughter could be less afraid. And in healing I'd also help heal my mom, and poor Alex, who will never unsee the shit he saw on the ice for the rest of his life, and everyone else who'd been through this with me.

This was the latest gift I received from the universe. Knowing that I had to drag my family and friends away from the fear as I recovered served to take the onus off me. In fact, it meant I didn't have to worry about me at all. I just had to keep getting better for my daughter first and foremost, then for my mom, then the rest of my family, because I knew that they would all start to heal because they would see me getting better. Every milestone I passed, no matter how big or small, would come with an image of their faces lighting up with their own joy, their own hope, and sometimes even a little relief.

All I had to do was keep getting better and everybody else could then heal and recover, too. I was now an inhabitant on the easiest planet you could imagine.

The effect of the shared experience that came because of the incident expanded way beyond me. What happened to me happened to a lot of people; the incident became a collective experience; what I understood now was that I hadn't been alone on the ice, and it hadn't just been Alex and Rich and Barb. All the people I loved and who loved me had been there with me. My recovery would become a collective healing. My getting better is my family getting better . . . together. If I was able to hang my hat on milestones, both physical and emotional, those milestones, no matter how small or seemingly insignificant, would naturally outweigh the tombstone and the wake of despair it leaves behind.

"Milestones over tombstones" became an inner mantra in my recovery.

So that second night I could see that my one-way road of recovery made my life very simple: Get better. Be stronger. Receive love. Find joy. Push to be tougher, faster, better than before.

I'd accept nothing less.

*   *   *

From the beginning, I was encouraged to move my body, especially where the breaks and the surgeries affected my mobility.

"Motion is lotion," one doctor told me. Scar tissue sets in very quickly and can be forever damaging to the body's mobility. When it came to specifically rehabilitating my left leg spiral fracture, with the titanium rod, plates, nails, and screws, it was imperative I stretch, move, flex, exercise, and create blood flow every day if I was to ever walk again. But every time I moved, my body responded by sending excruciating pain signals to my brain, exclaiming, "HEY—your leg is shattered over here . . . lay off." With every attempt at creating motion, I'd get a screaming pain signal to my brain, and the body was correct to send this signal to my brain, of course—it really is incredible how magnificent the human body is. It repairs itself constantly while also trying to protect itself.

But if I could zoom out and understand the hows and whys of pain, I might be able to reprogram my thinking and shift the way I received pain signals in my brain. Like time itself, physical pain is solely an earthly experience, not of the soul or spirit. So starting from this perspective, I discovered possibilities for pain management from what had previously seemed impossible. I had to be bold, consistent, and absolutely crazy ridiculous to redefine what pain was to me, so I started having serious, pointed conversations and drag-out arguments . . . with my leg.

It was bizarre, I know. I must have seemed like a lunatic, shouting directly at my leg.

"Stop telling me that you're broken, that you're hurt, and that I should be more careful!" I'd shout, like my leg was a scorned lover. "You, sir, have been replaced with something better and stronger than the bone, okay? So, pipe down, you son of a bitch!"

As I reprogrammed myself, step by step, I learned more and more and better understood my body and its limitations. So when I put my foot onto the ground and applied a little pressure, my pain nerves would light up like Christmas, and I would say out loud, biting my lip, "It's just nerves, they don't know any different. We're better than this, right?"

My body didn't understand I had been repaired and my bone replaced with a titanium rod and plates. My body had to learn that it is wrong and needs to redirect its comments to someone else who may or may not give a shit.

"Don't go away mad, sir, just go away . . . thank you," I'd say. "I officially UNSUBSCRIBE TO YOUR ISSUES! The best part of my day is when you're not in it," I'd rant, on and on.

My body was now a separate entity, a roommate if you will. And like a freeloading roommate, wanted or not, however hard I tried my body was nevertheless around, wasn't going anywhere, and was eating all my food and certainly not paying any rent.

I would practice this ridiculous perspective all through every day until my leg would actually listen.

"I'm trying to help us all out here," I'd regularly tell my leg, "so if you keep screaming at me, I am going to simply lop you off and hobble my way around just to shut you up. You understand me?"

Through the practice of removing my body and leg from my consciousness and making them characters on the same team, working toward the same goal (moving, walking, exercise), I was able to identify different nerve pains, and found new ways to interpret nerve pain signals in my brain. Often I was able to simply reduce them to being like an iPhone notification, which I could then just swipe away.

It took time and courage and a dash of insanity to build this accord, to change how my body receives and understands pain, but this was the basis of what I came to describe as the Agreement. But once the Agreement was in place—an agreement that allowed both parties to be heard, understood, and then kindly told to fuck off—pain simply became a notification in my brain. I can honor what my body has to say and certainly have a quick look, and then just as quickly swipe the notification away, and my pain goes along with it.

Pain is my bitch; I own it. It doesn't own me or dictate my spirit. Being human is simple at times. Pain is just nerve pathways, which are language. Pain still exists, but instead of "pain" I use the word "discomfort," or "stiffness," which doesn't sound as painful. When we switch our dialogue and definitions we can trick our pain center.

I have a deep understanding of what physical pain actually is—it has been tested in every part of my body—but pain is the last thing that is scary to me. Pain is simply a language, a barometer, an overprotective parent smothering its child with love and, like all languages, nothing is absolute and everything is open to interpretation. This is how I shut pain down and continue to work every day. Remember this: "It" only has value if *you* give it value (the variable "it" is wide open). This is manifestation DNA.

Creating these new neuro pathways gets easier if strictly continued for twenty-eight days.

Many things in our lives abide by the same twenty-eight-day cycle. The moon's cycle, twenty-eight days; desquamation (the natural sloughing of our skin, where new skin cells push out the old cells), twenty-eight days; the menstrual cycle, twenty-eight days; and neuro pathways that create habitual patterns are also created in twenty-eight days. New and positive habits are tough to create at first, but my body and mind conspired to make those good habits almost purely reflexive in time, just like breathing. Breathing, being reflexive, does not usually require any thought whatsoever because it is controlled by the autonomic nervous system. But conscious breath is something very different—I call it breathing with intention. Think of how your magnificent body reminds you of intended breath when you yawn. We do not yawn because we are tired; we yawn because our bodies require more oxygen, so we become our body's puppet and yaaaaaaaawn, inadvertently stretching our mouths agape like a goofy primate (and usually at the most inappropriate times and in the most inappropriate places).

So it would take twenty-eight days to reprogram my relationship to pain. I'd take any and all the help I could get.

*   *   *

With the coming days of recovery all in front of me, I was now going to will my mind and body back together. A positive mindset had always gotten me through my lows and my setbacks. It's no exaggeration to say that the road to recovery looked easy to me because it was a one-way road. There could be no distractions. One direction, one purpose. Don't just get back to level, but aim always to be *better* than before.

Belief and love and · excellence and failure and struggle and perseverance—these were my watchwords. There would be plenty of reasons to NOT go the extra mile in my recovery, but I chose instead a twenty-four-hour-a-day mindset to push myself. I could look at all of this as a positive decision or a necessity—either way, it had to be impervious to failure.

Over and over in the coming months I'd think, *Milestones are way better than a tombstone.* I would constantly set goals to hit, would mark progress, however small, and never judge even the simplest of tasks as not worthy of my effort. Sitting up? Opening my mouth fully? Peeing in a toilet instead of a jar? All these milestones and so many others I held to be as important as running a 4.5-second 40 meters.

There was to be no hierarchy of recovery, because I was determined to avoid being self-serving—I knew in my heart that I was recovering for others, not myself. Though feeding the ego can feel good in a temporary way, in the end it's fruitless, because it fails to acknowledge the collective energetic experience we are *all* a part of, a shared reality that will pull us through to a higher success if we get out of our own way.

So, would you rather contribute or vampire your way through life? I knew what the answer was for me.

It was the easiest question I ever asked myself.

*   *   *

There were times I got so high from the combination of opioids for pain and benzos for sleep that I was convinced the curtains in my bedroom were talking to me, and me to them.

Of course we were chatting—they were my buddies! We could talk about everything and anything. I remember one night telling them all about going hiking with my dad in Yosemite as a kid. Yosemite is only two hours east of Modesto, and I just can't think of a more awe-inspiring place—the granite cathedrals and glacial lakes, the sweeps of mountains and the smallest wildflowers, all underline how insignificant we humans are, and how pointless our stress and fears can be when faced with the magnitude and endless age of a 2,000-foot stone face in the morning sunlight. As my dad and I hiked, we talked, and he instilled in me the basis of whatever emotional intelligence I carry with me to this day. On those walks we'd talk religion, and philosophy, and life, and music.

One morning, I also told the curtains about the time my dad offered Kym and me two choices: Disneyland or the Doobie Brothers in San Francisco. It was no contest: Disneyland would always be there, but who knew how long the world would have the dulcet, back-of-the-throat tones of Michael McDonald?

When the curtains didn't respond, Jamie Foxx did. He was in my room quite a bit (he wasn't); we talked about this and that (I talked, he didn't say much, because he wasn't really there); we went snowmobiling together (we didn't—for a start, there's no snow in Southern California).

I wonder when he had his own medical issues a couple of months later if he talked to me, too? I hope I was there for him.

My mom or Kym or whoever was with me at the time would hear me chattering away and think, *Jeremy's just* tripping *right now.* Eventually I'd fall asleep, and someone would say, "Maybe we should dial back those meds—we don't want to lose him."

I couldn't find a single comfortable position to rest in, either; I was still leaning over to pee in a little jar; and when we got behind on the meds, and I didn't sleep, I faced a long-ass day. If I was lucky enough to get ten or twelve hours of sleep, I was rocking, doing therapies every day, doing all my workouts at 100 percent. But if I got behind the meds, or I just had a really shitty night's sleep . . .

. . . I remember the birds. They would be pecking at my bedroom window because they'd see their own reflection and think it was a competitor—it was nesting season by this point—and they kept me awake, their pecking worse than any nurse needing blood. *Peck peck peck*, interrupting my sleep. There was only one thing for it.

I asked Alex to go find my BB gun. He hesitatingly brought it to me, and I sat there in my wheelchair, my BB gun across my lap, just ready to lay waste to those fucking idiot house finches.

Fortunately, before I could blow a hole in my window, Alex put a row of spikes up, and then Jeff got a bunch of headshots of Hawkeye and made them into decals for the glass, thinking that might scare the birds away.

There I lay, nothing else to do but look at myself as Hawkeye on my bedroom window, my BB gun unused, watching those motherfucking birds, praying they'd let me sleep.

Some nights, when I did finally fall asleep, the crazy dreams would come. I've never been much of a dreamer, but in those first few weeks they would arrive in full Technicolor. They were most vivid right as I fell asleep. Sometimes I'd get night terrors, too, especially when I'd inadvertently fall asleep in the same position I'd found myself in right after the snowcat had left me shattered on the ice. Then, the terrors would ratchet up so high that eventually my violent clenching cracked a molar in the back of my mouth.

Beyond the parts of me I opted to not have surgery on, my mouth has been one of the constant issues since the incident. I had declined surgery on the fracture in my left hand. (What I actually said was, "Just leave it alone, it's fine!") My left wrist was also fractured. As for my left foot, there were the breaks in the two middle toes and a broken metatarsal—what they call a dancer's fracture—which was really distressing, and not just because I'd never be able to get on my tippy-toes ever again; it was also incredibly painful and debilitating. For a while it was thought my hearing was affected, too, but it turns out there was so much blood from the gash on my head caked in my ear that, once it was cleared out, everything came back to normal.

Then there was my right knee, which wasn't getting any better, and which would cause the greatest crisis of my recovery.

But my mouth was a disaster and having discomfort in the very place you eat, and talk, makes everything worse. My jaw, broken in three places, was held together with those Phillips-head screws and rubber bands. I could only slurp food for a while, which I hated—it's why I hate soup to this day. (Except for the butternut squash broth Kayla made for me and brought to the hospital—that tasted like nectar compared to institutional food.)

Despite my commitment to recovery, I was starting from way behind. My body was a hot mess; I was roadkill that made it. To this day I'm not sure the doctors caught every injury, and I don't think anybody ever will fully know all the things that got cracked or shattered or bent out of shape—it really doesn't matter. But my jaw . . . broken in three places, and my teeth forever misaligned, means it is never going to be the same ever again.

And yet I'm able to genuinely think, *What a blessing, what an honor. That's the worst of it.* For the rest of my life, I'll never be able to chew properly again, but who cares? Steaks aren't what they used to be; so what. I was determined to find something positive in everything. I could see perfectly, if not a little better; I had suffered no brain damage, no spinal break; eventually I'd be able to walk, then run. The chaos in my mouth is not something anyone will ever see; the only scars on my body from the incident come from the surgeries. I have one tiny scar in the back of my head that you'd have to go looking for. But otherwise, I'm fucking great.

Still, my ribs and my breathing remained a challenge in those early days back at home. If you've ever had bruised or cracked ribs, and then sneezed or even just taken a deep breath? For me, the foothills of a sneeze could bring on full terror. And given that so much of my upper body was under repair, I couldn't move well, either. I wasn't that worried about my lower body—it could just hang there while the rest of me recovered. But when I had to move, it required my upper body and that was brutal.

But it fixed very quickly. Once I learned to unlock my bones—a process that could take up to an hour each morning—I could bring movement into my arms and I could slightly move myself up in the bed; then I could sit up, then turn, then get out of bed more easily. It felt like within a week or two after I'd gotten home I could get my arm to move more freely, which in turn unlocked the cracked scapula, and everything else started to free up.

But still my teeth were always a disaster. It's no exaggeration to say that it's chaos in my mouth. And that night terror that cracked my tooth—right at the root—delivered so much pain I couldn't bear it.

That particular night terror had happened because of what I'd found out about my knee.

*   *   *

It's safe to say my family has a lot of unresolved feelings about my knee.

What I'd feared was an ACL or MCL or very bad strain turned out to be something much worse. My knee had suffered a Hoffa fracture, a sort of north-south fracture that is usually only treatable with surgery. It may have been something that could have been picked up earlier at Cedars or in Reno, but it wasn't, and my family was deeply frustrated that now it had become such a major issue as it has been a load-bearing leg for my movement thus far.

I wasn't exactly thrilled, either.

I just didn't have the energy for another stretch in the hospital. Worse, the usual fix for a Hoffa fracture not only entails major surgery (the scar alone can be twelve inches long), but then it's six weeks back in a wheelchair, and then another twelve weeks of muscle and tendon recovery. Surgeons would have had to reach under and pin the bone and honestly, though I'm tough, I didn't think I could be *that* tough all over again. Had I found my limit? I was pretty sure I didn't have this surgery in me.

I started telling anyone who'd listen, "Let's just lop the entire limb off so I can peg leg it and live a pirate life. Get me a ship and a parrot and I'll be fine."

The stress of waiting on whether I needed that surgery brought me deeper terrors at night than ever before, all of which led to that broken tooth. I just couldn't face starting over, and I don't think I would be the same man I am today if I had had to go back into Cedars for that surgery. I truly don't think I would have had the same verve, the same fight.

The wait was agonizing; it was the darkest of times. And then miraculously the surgeons said that the break was one millimeter—*one millimeter*—shy of needing surgery.

Every single tear I shed that day was from the pure joy of not having to have more surgery, for not having to take a massive step backward in my recovery. And then on top of that good fortune, I was lucky enough to find a dentist who agreed to fix my tooth in the late hours.

After that, it was all gravy, all beautiful tears.

But that "cut-off-my-leg-let-me-live-a-pirate-life" dark humor once again had a serious purpose. I was always determined to find a positive outcome to what I was going through, even if it meant losing a leg and making light of it. My superpower, probably before the incident but certainly after it, was, "How do I not live in agony but find joy?" If the number one directive in our lives was to look for and find joy, I wonder what our lives would look like. The only joy I had to look for and find was the joy that came from getting better, whatever it took.

But despite that perspective, bad weeks still came and went. The time waiting for the knee surgery decision was perhaps the most stressful. My jaw was still banded shut, but it was the tooth pain . . . those nerves in your head, the ones that most of us can relate to. It was a different pain from what I had experienced and I was still taking all those medications (opioids for pain, gabapentin for nerve pain). There was no swiping this pain notification away.

And then I decided I had to get off those pain meds.

*   *   *

I hated how the meds made me feel. Now that I was out of the hospital, I just wanted to rush back into a sense of normal, a normal that didn't involve chatting with curtains or an absent Jamie Foxx.

Once my tooth pain had been alleviated, I figured I didn't need pain meds at all. But me being me, I decided to go cold turkey.

I went from eighty to forty, then down to zero, all in one go.

Jesus, I suffered. I want to say that was the worst suffering of all, but it was just very different from anything else I went through. For about thirty-six hours I was crying and shivering, uncontrollable tears, doing everything I could to just calm down. I'd be doing my workouts with Christopher and just not be able to stop crying the entire time. Shivering, cold, frozen, back on the ice . . . By the end of the thirty-six hours everything felt very cold because now I could feel temperature more. I was always in heating blankets and found myself very sensitive to touch. I could feel my nerve endings once again. (Did I mention I also went cold turkey off the gabapentin, too—I'd taken the drug for anxiety, but I didn't feel like it did much for me, so I binned that at the same time.)

Right after I was done, I called my doctor.

"What's wrong with me?" I said. "I'm crying and shivering . . ."

"What's *wrong* with you?" he said, incredulous when I told him what I'd done. "Where do I start? First, you don't go cold turkey off these meds. They take about two weeks to safely stop—no one goes cold turkey."

"Well, I'm basically off them now," I said. "I haven't taken them in four days."

"Maybe you should still take a small dose now and then?" he said.

"I'm already past the crying and the hard part."

"So take something if you need them to sleep. There's nothing wrong with taking five, or even ten, to get you a night's rest."

So occasionally I did take a small dose here and there, but once I got over the hump, it was all pretty much smooth sailing. Every morning it felt like I was ninety years old, but I had strategies to get back to my actual fifties. I'd utilize a lot of vibration to get blood flowing through my body—vibrating plates or rollers and guns, all to get my body moving and to avoid blood clots. And heat was always good, too, hot, hot baths, 135, 140 degrees.

Initially it would take an hour to even get out of bed, and then after about a week it would take maybe forty-five minutes, and by the end of a month half an hour. Eventually I got to the point where I was out of bed immediately, but I'd still need a cane to get to the bathroom, even though I was now walking as much as possible.

I was Benjamin Buttoning from a ninety-year-old man in the morning to maybe a fifty-year-old man by the end of the day.

I had very, very specific goals I set for myself, and as I've said I used my daughter as the motivation for them because she was scared, and I couldn't live with that. Not that I didn't give a fuck about standing up and walking for myself—but I knew if I said to her, "I'm going to stand up on my own without anything, by your birthday in late March," then I had reason to do it faster because it wasn't just on my shoulders alone.

I had so many people to be accountable for. I screwed up their lives, but here's a way I could measure their recovery: by measuring my own. When I get better, they get better.

So here we go. Next milestone. Bring it.

*   *   *

If I was ever tempted to think I'd been through the worst, my recovery had a wonderful knack of reminding me to not let my guard down.

As I've said, to fix my jaw, I'd had screws placed in bone with elastic bands attached to keep everything together while it all healed.

Maybe six to seven weeks into my recovery, it was finally time to remove the screws and bands so I could start eating solid food.

I don't know why I thought there would be another way to do it other than the one that was being suggested as I sat in the doctor's office in Century City in Los Angeles. I never really thought about stuff until it was in front of me because I had so many things to worry about. So when faced with any procedure I always tended to be sort of wide-eyed about it until it actually happened.

When the day came for the screw removal I just thought, *Okay, we're going to take these out today.* I was more excited about not wearing the rubber bands than worried about how they would take out the screws.

Perhaps I should have mentally prepped a bit more for this one. Or at the very least thought to ask how it's done.

But here I was.

The problem was explained to me. I'd been sedated so many times and so deeply in the recent past that the surgeon said it would be best to just stick with *topical* numbing to get the screws out—that was the first sign that I was descending into some kind of medieval madness. I think the actual words the doctor said were, "Surgery would be worse. Just bear with us while we take those four screws out of your face."

Just bear with us . . . Hold on a second—*topical* numbing? There are four Phillips-head screws in my face. Because I'd failed to give serious thought as to how they would be removed, imagine my surprise and horror when the doctor reached into what can only be described as his toolbox and brought out a Phillips-head screwdriver.

(You might want to have that stiff drink for the next bit.)

The first screwdriver didn't quite fit the screws in my face, so he reached for a bigger one. What is this man about to do? Is he really going to . . . ?

An image of him wandering down aisle 31 of a Home Depot, looking for the right screwdriver, flashed across my brain. Other things flashed, too, words mostly, like "this motherfucker!" and "ain't no fucking way!"

The screwdriver didn't even look *medical* grade. It literally looked like a screwdriver you'd get in any Home Depot, probably because IT WAS A SCREWDRIVER YOU'D GET FROM ANY HOME DEPOT. And he was really going to remove screws from my face with this thing? Did he even *sterilize* it first?

He asked me to remain calm.

Ha, this motherfucker . . .

He applied a topical numbing drop to the gums around the screws.

And then he got to work on the first of the four screws embedded deep in my sorry face.

This is what horror films are made of.

First thing to tell you about the process is that just like a horror film, someone is going to die in these first few minutes.

When you're unscrewing a screw from a two-by-four, it makes a peculiar squeaking sound. Apparently, the same is true with your face.

"AH! MUVA FUVA!" I scream as he holds my mouth and my jaw with his hand and uses one thumb underneath my upper lip to push it up to gain access. He continues to methodically torque and twist. *Schreeeek! Schraaaawch!*

Ooooh this is worse. It's like the sound of a front door to a very fucking haunted house.

I'm trying to keep still, all the while the nasty squeaking sound and vibration rattle my brain to the brink of insanity. He may as well just slide that screwdriver up my nose to my frontal lobe and scramble my brain, so I have no memory of him and this nightmare.

I think, *I'm actually going to knock this guy out; I'm gonna kill him. This is the worst thing that's ever happened to me in my life, and I was crushed to death by my snowcat!*

As he continues to unscrew, he displays a kind of Terminator face, doing his best to show no emotion. Perhaps this is because I am emoting enough for the both of us, but also it's because that's what doctors do. Then a more considerate thought wanders by—*This can't be any fun for him, either, right?*—but with one more slow twist, that thought is replaced by more expletives and images of homicide.

Finally, the first screw is out, and it is a considerably longer object than I had anticipated. The doctor then starts on the second, but he hasn't hit the gums around the screw with the topical numbing agent—he'd missed the mark and got the screw instead. I know this because . . . (please forgive me for the next few words) I can feel my gums twisting and lifting around the thread of the screw as he turns it.

By this point I'm making any and all noises to distract me not only from the squeaking sounds and the vibrations, but from some new and vivid images of twisting gums on metal. Then flashes of Laurence Olivier doing unsedated dentistry on Dustin Hoffman in *Marathon Man* run through my mind.

I'm haunted by this whole thing to this day, though I will say that after the first couple of screws, the other two were actually fine! I knew what to expect, at least, and he managed to get the numbing right.

And—upside!—no longer having screws and rubber bands in my mouth meant I could have my first real meal since the accident: a Burrito Supreme from Taco Bell.

Hell yeah, I'm doing that.

*   *   *

Sometimes I'll have daydreams about the things I've been through, and I'll glaze over until I'm able to replace the terrible images in my head. When something pops up, I just replay it, but just as quickly I find myself thinking, *I've come so far.* Those images work like a barometer, a progress report of how far I've come or even, *How did I get through that? Jesus!* Or else I get to reflecting on so many things that could have gone even worse.

I choose always to not curl up and hide.

During my recovery I was with someone every day, twenty-four hours a day, and we would talk about what happened all the time, so there was nothing buried, no stone unturned. I have control of how I feel, and I choose to think, *I'm so lucky.* I get to steer this thing, and not let it steer me. True, I could just go down a dark road like anybody, I suppose—I could say, "Why me?" or "I'm never going to be the same" or "I'm never going to be an actor ever again" or "Who's going to love me again?" But even saying these things feels so foreign to me.

They don't sound like me.

They don't sound like me at all.

*   *   *

About seven weeks after I left the hospital, when I was still mostly bed-bound, or else in a wheelchair, I decided it was time to hit a major milestone.

So that day, I struggled my way out of bed, out of my house, and into my car. Not for the first time I was so grateful it wasn't a stick shift—I was perfectly capable of driving with one leg, but definitely not with two. But I had a date that day with someone incredibly special, though she had no idea what was coming, and nothing was going to stop me.

That day, as Ava came out of school, her dad was there waiting for her in the driver's seat. It had taken me about an hour to get out of the house and into the car, but there I was.

She could not believe I was there.

I could not believe I was there.

But there we were, together, father and daughter, moving forward, inch by slow inch.

Picking Ava up that day gave me a huge boost of confidence. It made me feel like I was once again participating in the world. So even though I was pushing the envelope, it was absolutely necessary. No doctor would ever have thought to sign off on that drive, that struggle out of my house and into the car.

That's why I didn't even ask.

And anyway, my daughter had kept her promise. She had waited for me. And here I was.

11

WHITE NOISE

By Good Friday, April 7, 2023—exactly three months after I'd left Reno to head south to Cedars-Sinai—I was well enough to spend a day at Magic Mountain, the Six Flags amusement park an hour north of Los Angeles.

I was now able to get around using a cane, though I couldn't get very far—maybe one hundred feet without getting bone-tired or falling into intense pain. But still, with the help of one of those little scooters folks use at Walmart and Costco, I was able to get myself around a fair amount of the two-hundred-acre property and to ride many of the rides.

Just three months after the incident I found myself hurtling down Full Throttle and Apocalypse and Goliath, whooping and hollering, Ava by my side, my mom down on the ground looking scared half to death.

I'd been walking on a treadmill for about a month by this point, as well as riding a stationary bike and working hard on all the other rehab machinery Christopher Vincent had installed in my home. But getting out to Magic Mountain was an even more important milestone for me.

I've always loved roller coasters; I'm one of those people who when adrenaline kicks in is at their most comfortable. Some people run from the rush, or are made uncomfortable by it, or hate it—I'm not that person. Who knows if it's genetic, but I think my "fight" reaction when faced with fears helped me on the ice, though it wasn't the first time my positive use of adrenaline had given me an advantage.

A few years ago, I was having lunch at the Saddle Ranch Chop House on Sunset Boulevard in West Hollywood when a guy started to choke on his food. The man was clearly unhoused—no shirt, overalls, poignantly hiding out in the corner having his meal. The kindly staff had given the man a burger to eat, but it had gone down the wrong way, and sadly none of the other customers seemed compelled to help, given that his personal hygiene was not the greatest. But my adrenaline kicked in and I automatically rushed over to where he was convulsing and performed the Heimlich maneuver on the guy. It was a knee-jerk reaction to stress, and was something anyone would (and maybe should) have done. But the whole incident made me realize that all my work on facing fears and gaining information had come together to give me an advantage over people who might otherwise hide or freeze. I had learned to conspire with my body to overcome a natural fear reaction to get to the point where I wasn't afraid of much at all anymore. I know my body is still going to react to frightening stimuli—that's such an innate part of human DNA that it's only freaks of nature who are able to turn it off altogether—but I also know even with a spike of cortisol, I'll still be able to separate myself enough from my own biology to take decisive and, in the case of the man in the diner, lifesaving action.

Once again, my reaction was all about data, about understanding that so much of fear and inertia is simply a lack of information. As soon as you understand something, your fears can lessen, and you can take decisive action.

That was exactly what happened on the ice for me right after the incident. Once I could get my breathing corralled, then I could start to take an inventory and make an on-the-fly plan for survival. As ever with me, the truth was that once I had information, fear reduced—not eliminated, just lessened to the point where I could function and, hopefully, come out alive.

It was the same thing that day at Magic Mountain as we came barreling down the eighty-five-mile-per-hour, 255-foot drop of Goliath, screaming our heads off. I knew we were safe, that this was just a massive adrenaline spike (just as I knew that Ava had worn extra socks that day to be tall enough to ride Goliath with me).

Though my bones were no longer broken at this point, I still had lots of healing to do inside me that day at Magic Mountain. I was able to conspire with my mind to lessen the pain to a slight discomfort in order to share something important with my family. This was a key day in showing everyone around me—and myself—that my recovery was surging forward, that I'd not only survived but that I could get back to a life that included doing things like riding roller coasters with my daughter, as I always had before.

By this point in my recovery, I was marshaling anything I could to get my body back into a vessel that didn't hamper my ability to live the life I wanted to live. But nothing was going to stop me. And beyond that, something else had happened in the three months since the incident that had given me immense hope that the incident had fundamentally shifted the world around me. When I was out in public, people saw me in a new light.

*   *   *

I feel only gratitude for the opportunities my job has given me, but it's not always easy being a public figure. I realize this sounds like the tiniest violin playing, but I'd noticed that there were times when people thought I was their property, pushing me for selfies when I was just trying to have a private dinner with my daughter or a friend. Being in the Marvel universe, and working on *Mission: Impossible*, had only exacerbated this sense that I no longer belonged only to those closest to me but to anyone who had a cell phone.

But after the incident, this was no longer the case. I noticed the shift first at Magic Mountain. Where previously my wandering around an amusement park might have been one long photo op for fans—and therefore not that much fun for my family who were having to share me with the whole world—now there was a compassion and respect that were palpable. All I got that day was good wishes, thumbs-up, and a respectful distance that I found very moving. And then it struck me: Perhaps I could now be well known for something other than my job; perhaps now I could be more famous for what I'd overcome than for wearing tights and carrying a bow and arrow. Maybe I could now be notable for being the man that I am rather than the roles I play.

That day at the park, not a single person asked for a selfie. Instead, as I passed by, folks would call out, "Good on you, man!" and "Glad you're here!" On roller coasters my fellow thrill-seekers would yell, "We fucking love you, Renner—so happy you're alive." It felt like I was being seen for who I was: just a regular guy, a father, son, sibling, friend, rather than a generator of headlines.

But it wasn't just amusement parks. Before the incident, the only thing that ever gave me unbearable anxiety was airports. Traveling alone through an airport was a super-toxic thing for me; I'd be inundated with people wanting pictures and hugs and autographs. Sitting by myself, waiting for a flight, I would find myself in a state of deep anxiety, so much so that I'd often have to hide in a bathroom stall to get some peace. This led to me even eating my lunch in the stall, pasta plates on the toilet, hoagies on the throne. Back out in the departures area I'd have to wear sunglasses to be blind, headphones to be deaf, just so I could get a moment's peace.

But recently I flew to and from Mexico alone, and the experience was completely different. It wasn't just that people treated me with respect—I also found myself more open to interactions that previously I might have avoided. One family in particular stays with me. Right after passing customs back into the United States I found myself standing with a Mexican family—mom and dad, and a whole slew of kids under eight years old.

The children were too young to know who I was, though the mom said, sweetly, "I know your name . . ."

"I'm Jeremy," I said.

"*Avengers!*" she said.

And with that we all gathered for a group photo, taken by an immigration officer. It was such a beautiful, innocent moment, matched by so many other interactions where someone would whisper in my ear or simply touch my shoulder, saying, "We're happy you're here." Almost every interaction now is to do with the incident and the fact that I survived it. What used to be toxic is now human; what used to be soulless is now intimate. And I am more available and less reactive, too.

In fact, I was starting to feel the first inklings of a kind of profound peace, a peace that had sometimes escaped me up to that point. Don't get me wrong: I'd been happy before the incident. For a decade or more I'd lived a lucky, glorious life, a great life, and whatever happened in my career, my family was always the bedrock of that happiness, so I was a blessed man. But now to be recognized for something else? I'd been trying to see and witness people my entire life—it's what I feel like I do for a living. I always do my best to remain curious, to pay attention, and to witness people. I have been so lucky to have developed positive, deep relationships with friends, and I hope that's because I pay attention. The people around me know that I'll show up for them, they know that I'll do whatever they need when they need anything. I may not say as many words as others, I may have been out in the yard sneaking a cigarette to get some alone time in the past, but when it matters, I deeply pay attention and do shit to help those around me. I try always to really see somebody, to go deep, to understand.

Now, as my family and I walked around Magic Mountain, it felt like the love I'd tried to give to my friends and family was being reflected back, genuinely and with no agenda, and by strangers.

This would prove to be an extraordinary sea change in my life. A new portal was opening for me, one in which I could use my so-called fame to make real differences in people's lives. If I could effect real change in the world around me, surely that was the central lesson of being spared that morning on the ice. If I could walk in public and have only love and good wishes offered to me, then it was surely my job to reflect that love back, and double down on what was most fundamental about the incident and its aftermath: the triumph of love over death.

*   *   *

Still, the spinning wheels of show business continued to turn, and I knew I'd need to get back to work at some point. But even then, I sensed that those wheels were now turning in a different way.

With the premiere of *Rennervations* on the horizon, I wanted to do as much publicity for it as I could so that people would know to tune in. Initially, Disney had quite rightly wondered if they should delay the show given the seriousness of what I'd been through, thinking that maybe I wouldn't be physically up to publicizing a TV show. But we'd all worked so hard on the show, it felt even more relevant now that my place in the culture had begun to shift, and I wanted this show to be seen. (I also wanted the world to see that I was doing well and that it's possible to overcome the worst of odds.) So on Monday, April 10, three days after Magic Mountain, I headed to *Jimmy Kimmel Live!* to do my first public appearance since the incident.

As I walked out that night carrying my cane, I was once again overwhelmed by the reaction of people, so much so that I found myself doing a brief dance before I sat down. Looking out at the crowd, I sensed that what I'd been through was way more important than who I'd played in movies—and there, at the end of the front row, sat my mom, Kym, Kayla, Nicky, and Alex, their smiles wider than a mile. "They've been at my side the entire time," I told Jimmy as we chatted. And did I sense in those smiles that they were beginning to heal, too?

*   *   *

A few days later still, on Thursday, April 13, we held a premiere for *Rennervations* at the Eldorado Hotel and Casino in downtown Reno. It was a chance to show the community some of the exciting things we'd been doing to repurpose vehicles for communities just like Reno, and to say thank you to everyone for all their love and support during and since the incident.

A week earlier, *Jeremy Renner: The Diane Sawyer Interview—A Story of Terror, Survival and Triumph* had aired. Diane had not only interviewed me and my family about the incident but had tracked down Dr. Althausen and some first responders and Barb and Rich, all of whom had been so fundamental to my survival. Before then I had never thought to make a lot of the incident public—I was honestly just trying to move on, and I had so much healing left to do. But just as I'd been floored by the look on the faces of my actor friends, looks that had revealed to me the true extent of what had happened to me, so attention seemed to come my way without me even trying and underscored that far from the incident being a private disaster, it was becoming a tale of survival that the wider world had paid real attention to.

From genuinely thinking I'd continue to recover and eventually everyone would move on, the truth was that what I went through was clearly resonating beyond me and my family. That's why it felt natural to continue sharing the recovery process because it really wasn't about me and what I'd been through anymore—it was about how anyone, if they combine information with love, can survive and even flourish when the worst things happen.

I'd understood Disney's reluctance to move forward with the agreed timeline for *Rennervations*, but in the end I found myself screaming at them. "Not a chance!" I said to Disney, that bastion of family entertainment. "I look fine! I'm going to be able to walk that red carpet. We worked too damn hard to shelve the show." In my mind we had addressed the incident publicly with the Diane Sawyer interview, and now we could air *Rennervations* on Disney+, and then the summer would show up and life would just continue.

I was wrong about the last bit. The ripple effect from the incident just kept getting wider and wider. There was now no way I could just brush it away and pretend it didn't happen, or even downplay the deeper meanings of it. I started to hear from so many people who'd been through their own trauma: They'd lost a limb or had torn up their knee or had a terrible accident of their own. One guy, a pro soccer player who'd had a similar tibia injury, started messaging me, saying he was inspired by me, whatever the heck that means. But I'll take it—if it meant being able to look outside myself for the positives, to create a deeper narrative for something as seemingly banal as an accident clearing snow, then I was all in.

*   *   *

Once the premiere of *Rennervations* was over that night in Reno, I was leaving the auditorium when I thought I heard a woman's voice call my name. People shout my name all the time at public events, but something in the tone of *this* voice stopped me in my tracks.

Earlier, as the event had started, Barb Fletcher had been trying to find somewhere to sit, but the place was packed. Kym and Alex had happened to bump into her and promptly brought her to sit with the family, because she *was* family now. Later, as Barb had been on her way out of the auditorium, she'd seen me leaving and had wanted to say hello but I was surrounded by a scrum of people.

But her voice had stopped me cold. There she was, the woman who had ministered to me for forty-five minutes a few months earlier, a true angel who had put aside her own heartache to help keep me alive. Our eyes met; I pushed through the crowds. I didn't say anything because there were no words—instead I just grabbed her and wrapped her up in the strongest hug my still shattered body could manage. I wasn't going to let go; Barb, in turn, put her head on my shoulder and I heard her say something.

"It just wasn't your time," she was whispering. "You do a lot of good for people, a lot of good for this community. That's why you're still here."

There was nothing I could say back to her; it was too momentous a meeting to be adequately expressed in language.

Fortunately, Ava said everything I wish I could have said. She saw me being hugged by Barb and ran over to hug her, too.

"Thank you so much for saving my dad," my amazing daughter said.

This was the first time that I had met my neighbor Barb after the incident, and I held on to her, and I didn't let go. I sobbed so deeply with love and gratitude from every cell in my body, from my soul, from my entire family. This now was the most vulnerable and profoundly thankful I had felt since the incident. Barb broke down, too, crying into my shoulder, as Ava, the angel I was living for, wrapped her wings around both of us.

*   *   *

Physically, I was probably only "an eighth of the way there," as Christopher Vincent told *People* magazine around that time. "We've only scratched the surface on the amount of work he's got left," he said. "Once the bones all heal, then we can really start to fire up the muscles, we can really see what joints are damaged and what nerves are really damaged. We have to build back the strength."

Still, the body is a wonderful instrument. Yes, you have to work it and you have to push it, but if you tear a muscle and work it, it will come back stronger. And that's what was happening to me. My family started to notice that I appeared even fitter now than I had been before the incident.

But the body was only half of the equation—I knew my brain could still screw everything up, so a huge part of my focus and drive was mental. Recovery is lonely; no matter how much love I was surrounded by (and I had more love than you can imagine), it was still just me on the treadmill, or on the stationary bike, and it was still just me wading through rivers of pain at night. All I could do was "gamify" my recovery, giving myself challenges to get better than I had been the day before or the hour before, urging myself to take the next step, just as, those months earlier on the ice, I'd urged myself to breathe out so I could breathe air back in.

I was so focused, and what could have been endlessly difficult became easier when I realized how simple the task was. If today I'm just sitting up this much, or raising my arm this much, or getting out of a chair this quickly, then to better that achievement the following day meant that I didn't have to look too far ahead.

My recovery, too, had loaned me a much simpler way to live, which made it a wonderful blessing for a busy guy like me, because all the busy-ness went away. When Jimmy Kimmel asked me what the "best thing" was about the incident, I'd joked that "when I woke up, the first thing I thought about, my first conscious thought, was, *Holy hell, my calendar's freed up for the rest of the year!* Yeah! I was making so many plans; I was going to buy a boat, gonna go live in Mexico . . . my year was pretty jammed up until I got crushed!"

There was a profound truth to the joke I'd shared with my friend on TV. What had disappeared was the white noise in my life. In this new reality, I could so clearly see what I needed without extraneous and pinching distractions. Everything had been boiled down for me, dis-tilled, brought to an essence. It made making decisions so much easier than before.

I now have such clarity with the white noise gone. Everything I do now is purposeful, everything's intended. Before, the white noise could dominate my decision-making and blur what I want to give value to in my life. Will I concern myself with exciting ideas of the future or spend more time presently because I already have all I want in life? I think about nothing save my next breath, because to this day I still have to fight for each of those. There's a silence in me now, one that has given me a crystal-clear vision of who I am and what I want to do with my life.

And with that silence comes an even clearer sense of the reality of how deeply I love and care for the things I deeply love and care for—now, I focus and surround myself with *only* those things. This superpower of clarity is amazing. I no longer think, *What should I do next as an actor?* I don't give a hoot about anything besides my physical health and my family, because the healthier my body gets, the more I am allowed to deepen my emotional and spiritual health so I can fully experience life with the people around me. The white noise of what I want to eat for my next meal is gone. What do I think of this shampoo compared to that shampoo, this moisturizer versus that moisturizer? I don't care about anything except taking care of my physical health.

Now, every room I walk into I carry all my injuries, all my once-broken bones, all my titanium. But instead of seeing all this as an ailment, I see it as a superpower. Healing has let me ask, "What do I want to focus on? What do I no longer want to run from?" Answering those questions has helped me focus on what I want in my life and get rid of the things I don't want in my life.

I've been "reduced"—actually, it's "raised"—to being an eight-year-old again, and it took a 14,000-pound machine to roll all that crap out of me. And knowing that I would come out the way I came out? It may sound perverse to say it, but I'd do it again in an instant. Knowing I'd get all the gifts I received from the planet, from my loved ones, from myself . . . yes, I'd do it again. I'm not going to, you understand, but let me be clear: I would highly recommend getting run over by a snowcat if you could guarantee that your life could turn out the way mine has in the last year. The gifts that have come from surviving the incident are just about greater than the pain I caused my mom and my sister and my daughter, greater than the pain I incurred upon myself, and that will be true in perpetuity.

I hope I live a long time, but however long I have, that life is going to be a much simpler one, filled with love and honor and humility and gratitude. I tried to live that way before, and sometimes succeeded, but with the white noise out of the way, now these things are all I've got.

People around me say things like, "Jeremy is softer, now," and it's true. It's because I don't have to fight off so much "grizzly shit," as I call it. They say I seem happier, healthier, a "better version of himself." I'm not so busy with life and all the busyness life entails; I've pulled myself from the world a little bit so I can heal. And I've calmed down.

"He glows," as my sister Nicky recently put it. My healing body is fueling a softer, more peaceful kind of place for me to inhabit. Knowing that, of course I'd do it again. I don't want to have to, but if we can change our perspective on even the worst things we go through, then the pain of life won't be wasted. It can be fuel to burn up all the waste, a button we can press to silence the white noise and live the life we've always wanted to.

*   *   *

This is the best time of my life; it's never been better. Being on a very clear path is something I'd wish for anyone. When we travel on unpaved paths in our youth—or whenever we do so—we wonder if we'll ever see an open road where the life we want to lead is possible. No road is ever completely paved, never completely smooth. And I don't suspect smooth sailing for the rest of my life, either, but my path, at least, is pretty clear.

In the past, though I was so happy to be traveling the world as an actor, it also meant I was away from my family, and especially Ava, far too much. For so much of my life, my job had taken me away from the people I loved. Yes, I was doing something I loved, but it was a job I had to do alone. This could make me frustrated, and short-tempered, something of a cantankerous guy—I was doing the very thing that I loved to do, but I wasn't getting to share it with anybody. Being away from my family sucked; even when I was able to focus on all the beautiful things that it gave me—the places I saw, the amazing people I met and worked with, the riches it provided—still I knew I was missing so much that was elemental to my happiness.

These days I can just work with people I love to work with. I think differently about everything now. My first question always is, "How can I capture more of the time I want?"

Underlying everything is that I don't want to be a spectator in my daughter's life, never want to merely sit in the stands and watch her play some sport; I'd much rather *do* stuff with her. After I missed her first birthday because I was in London working with Tom Cruise, I vowed that would never happen again, and even before the incident I had been making different decisions. I remember saying to my manager that Ava has to see my face every morning when she wakes and see my face every night before she goes to bed—that was an emotional decision that also affected the work I did, but no one was going to pressure me to not be the father I wanted to be. That was the main reason I stepped away from the *Avengers* movies (that and the tights—no one wants to see a fifty-something man in tights). I've turned down more money than I'll ever be able to make, and I'm fine with that.

Plus, I know I can live happily on five dollars a month. Donut holes aren't so bad.

Now, after the incident, I am even more adamant that any work decision I make is completely informed by my need to be with my family.

And it's not just Ava—my mom had me when she was eighteen and never got to see the world. That, too, was about to change. I agreed to do *Knives Out 3* for two reasons: one, I love Rian Johnson, the director, and his team of producers, and my costars (for a start, getting to work with one of my idols, Glenn Close, was too good to pass up, and another vow I'd made was only to work with people I cared about going forward). And two, as it was filming in London during the summer, I would get to take Ava and my mom, and whoever else in the family wanted to go, to see Europe.

*   *   *

The filming of *Knives Out 3* would be on tap for 2024—for now, on November 14, 2023, people on Instagram would have perhaps seen a video of a man running down and back up his driveway. On the way down he did some lateral steps, swinging his arms back and forth, as though he was dancing to some internal music. The driveway had a significant grade, but there was a lightness to his dance, a sprightly step, a joy to it. At the bottom of the driveway he paused, out of breath—it looked like he was done. Then, with a slight smile at the camera, he got a second wind and high knee jogged back up the hill, arms pumping, just a middle-aged guy running up and down his driveway.

That man was me. The caption on the post read, "Today marks the day of 10 months of recovery . . . First attempt at any of this activity (especially at steep grade) and was brought to tears of joy, hopefulness, and gratitude for all your support along with my family and friends . . . I keep pushing for many reasons, but you are my fuel."

Not too many months earlier, doctors had told me I would never walk again, and even if I did, I'd walk funny. "For sure," they said, "you're never *running* again."

Now here I was, jogging up and down my driveway a week before Thanksgiving. Beyond the physical triumph of it, I felt a surge of confidence in my heart and brain, which felt even more meaningful than the actuality of running for the first time. The next step happens and then the next step happens, trail markers for my recovery. And before you know it, a man who should be walking funny is running.

I ran past the camera back toward my house, where, as ever, my family was waiting to greet me.

*   *   *

And then it was time to slay another dragon: I was going to get back on that snowcat and fire it up.

I was getting back on that thing because I was not going to let it haunt me. My mom had wanted to burn it, but I had long since decided that instead of a monster, the snowcat would become a beacon of the love that had deepened in my family.

Climbing back up into the cab was fine; firing it up was fine; simply moving it from one point to another was fine because I knew how to work it.

What was a bit unsettling, though, was jumping down off the snowcat and finding small pieces of my clothing still stuck in the tracks. There was part of my hat; there were strips of my clothes. The sheriffs had removed most of this stuff back when they'd impounded the machine during their pro forma investigation, but they had missed some of it, and here it was.

Those bits of clothing became another symbol of something profound. My body could actually survive after being dragged under and crushed by this machine. Standing once again on the tracks—the STOP button firmly pressed, the hand brake firmly applied—I thought, *Human body's an impressive piece of biology, man.*

And then I safely jumped down and headed up to the house.

CAMP RENNERVATION

I'll forever be in recovery; it never ends. But I accept that; I'm not whining about it. Given that I was past fifty, I already needed to pay a lot of attention to my body and my flexibility and my joints, so it's a blessing to now do it in a deeply responsible way and be excited about it.

But it's not always easy (and never painless). Going back to the set of *Mayor of Kingstown* to make season 3, as I did at the start of 2024, was probably even more physically challenging that I'd imagined it would be.

For a start, I tend to do my own stunt work, but would I even be able to perform effectively given my physical limitations? It turned out that the challenge was as much mental as it was physical. Rather than being worried about my strength, could I control my limbs given that I still had limited strength in the joints and muscles?

The first stunt I had to do on *Mayor* was to knock a couple of mobsters out on a set of wet steps. We'd set it up so that a stuntman could do the action if I wasn't up to it, but I ended up doing it and it went better and faster than we even had anticipated. In fact, even though I was only supposed to punch a guy, I ended up leaping and Superman-punching him. As I did so, in the distance I could faintly hear cheers coming from the director's tent off set. "The mayor is back!" someone said. "Jeremy is back!"

I got a lot of hope that day; I could still do the job, and it also meant the writers could write what they wanted to write (stage directions like, "Mike smashes bad guys," for example).

We shot that scene during the third week of filming (though it appeared in episode 1), when I was still pretty fragile. For a start it was freezing in Pittsburgh where we shoot the show—there was snow and ice on the ground, which is not good on my body. I found myself falling asleep on set, and there was a moment when the doctors thought I'd need to leave Pittsburgh altogether and head home to properly rest. Had we moved too quickly? Days on set can last fourteen hours, so we put a limit of eight hours on my schedule, which helped.

But the real issue was that my blood work was garbage. I couldn't convert anything I was taking into energy. I was always fatigued. My testosterone levels were at 200 when they're supposed to be around 1100. The transfusions and surgeries and all the damage from the incident had left me terribly depleted, and my body was working so hard to recover on a cellular level. Fortunately, they can quantify that process with weekly blood panels to see what the body is underproducing and overproducing, then figure out supplements and injections to improve my energy levels.

I was an ongoing science experiment. For example, we learned from the panels that my body reacts really well to testosterone injections. We discovered that I could take a relatively tiny amount and get great results—people take four times the amount that I take every week to get the same results I can get in ten days. But still, right before I'd headed to Pittsburgh to start season 3, I'd been both weak *and* gaining weight—I was working out four and five days a week to get ready for the filming, and I was still maybe thirty pounds heavier than I'd ever been. My organs had taken on all this fat to protect them after the trauma and wouldn't let it go. It was brutal.

To fix it, like the guy who went cold turkey off his meds, I fasted for four days, which shocked my body into eating the fat off all my organs.

I dropped fifteen pounds before I arrived in Pittsburgh on January 8, a year and a day after my first surgery at Cedars. I still struggled with my energy for most of the shooting, but by about the tenth week I was starting to feel much better.

What I'd learned was that it takes a lot longer to do what my mind still thinks is easy. My new body responds much more slowly than it once did, and I'm a little impatient with that, so I push it more and push it more and push it more. And then with that impatience comes dejection because it's a lot of hard work for zero fucking results.

But what else am I going to do? This is the one-way road I've been talking about. Of course, maybe one day I'll just burn out and become four hundred pounds even though I'm working out seven days a week and eating nothing but chicken breasts and broccoli. Broccoli and chicken breasts and a weight machine work for everybody else on the planet, but it just takes longer for me now, I guess. And it's not as if I'm trying to get muscle-bound. I simply need to gain strength for my joints so I can walk and run properly. I still have a way to go to train my brain to operate in this new reality, but all I have is time. It won't be squandered.

*   *   *

My mouth is a disaster, though; it's an absolute nightmare in there, my own private hell. Every time I'm talking, or eating, or sleeping, I want to scream inside because of the chaos in my mouth. My teeth will never line up properly again; one side got pushed so far offline by the snowcat and it's unfixable.

The other night, during a night terror, I must have been clenching and one of my teeth popped because of the misalignment of my jaw. It won't be the last time, and no, it's not a pleasant surgery to fix.

But I live with it—I'm not happy about it, but I live with it. I'm just glad I'm walking right now, so screw my mouth. Who cares? I really think that way. I don't love it, but I can live with it because I can *live*. I still have a smile. I don't look like a complete freak.

I refuse to give these private agonies too much energy because they really don't have that much value. There are so many other things to focus on. So many other things to focus on that have value and for which I'm grateful.

I got burnt yesterday out in the LA sun. It was the best day.

I'm grateful for sunburn now. Imagine that.

*   *   *

I'm not the only one feeling gratitude and great change in my life.

I was talking to Dave Kelsey recently, and this is what he said: "What happened has had such a profound impact on my perspective and approach to life. It has heightened my awareness to its fragility, and it's led overall to a deep, much deeper appreciation for every day. I've noticed that I'm just cherishing moments more, savoring experiences more deeply, and expressing gratitude all the time. It's strengthened my relationships and has served as a reminder just how important loved ones are. Now, I find myself prioritizing family and friends, spending really quality time with them, making a conscious effort to nurture and strengthen those relationships. I think I'm more empathetic, too."

As I've said over and over, this didn't just happen to me. It happened to everyone. Hearing Dave talk about how his life had changed was incredibly meaningful to me, and he wasn't the only one.

Rory Millikin had started to reevaluate and face some of his deepest feelings about his brother and it's underlined for him how our families are all that matters in the end.

Alex had come with me to Pittsburgh to work on the third season of *Mayor of Kingstown*, keeping me close, and me him, our mutual healing back and forth. Recently he said to me, "The whole time I've been healing, through it all, I've been healing *with* you. And it hasn't been something to hold me back. It's something to propel me forward. I can look at what happened and sometimes think, *Fuck, that's a bad memory, but I don't think it scarred me. It didn't scar me because of how you are.*"

My pal Jesse, the former firefighter who had gotten the awful call that paramedics had "done the best they could" for me, says this now: "What happened makes you really appreciate life and friends, everyone around you. You realize life is very short and can go away at any point. I don't know exactly what I'd do in the same kind of situation you found yourself in, but I know now that I'd be inspired to fight to stay alive." Jesse even went crazy and finally bought a boat he'd always promised himself—he called it *Risk Reward*.

As for my mom and Kym and Alex and Nicky and Kayla, the difference in their lives could be most easily seen on the banks of Lake Tahoe in the summer of 2024.

*   *   *

Fifteen months ago, I was dead, but when you conspire with the positive energy around you, you tend to attract more positive energy, and pretty much anything is possible. But first, you have to put yourself into positions that make you uncomfortable so you can grow, doing stuff that you're not necessarily good at.

For example, I'd never run a children's summer camp. Neither had my family and friends. But here we were on July 15, 2024—me, Alex, my mom, Kym, Nicky, Kayla, Rory, Dave, and so many others—watching as a couple of buses we'd rescued from the scrapyard came rolling into the 4-H Camp in Stateline, on the eastern shore of Lake Tahoe. (One of the buses was being driven by Jesse, whose boat was moored for the week at the water's edge so we could use it for the kids.)

The buses were filled with foster kids arriving for Camp Rennervation, which our foundation had put together to give these 110 children a chance at a bonding, uplifting week of love and fun. I had been building my field of dreams for a long time with Rennervation, but it had usually been me and maybe one other person, never really a full team. Now, everyone around me was uniting to make a difference. My sister Kym and one of my best girl friends, Shana Rogers, came together to run the foundation. Kym and Shana, along with my mom and my other siblings, threw themselves full-time into making this camp, and so many other initiatives, a place where kids who really need it get support, attention, and something special they can take with them through what are often tough circumstances. In Washoe County alone, where Lake Tahoe sits, there are more than six hundred children in foster care at any one time, and nearly half a million nationwide—an obscene number—and we just wanted to do our part to make their lives better, even if only for a week.

Being in the public eye has given me one thing of real importance: I have the privilege to be able to provide opportunities and share positive experiences with kids. It's a blessing to have an impact; I like to think that this alone is another one of my superpowers.

I first truly realized this superpower/blessing when I dropped off my daughter in kindergarten. *Avengers: Endgame* had just come out and as I walked away from leaving her at the door, I started to hear my first and last names being called. I turned and saw a bunch of kids running at me. I knew I only had three minutes to drop Ava off and leave the campus before I got locked in, but there I was with thirty kids running at me with cell phones, and no one was shouting "Hawkeye!"—they were all yelling "Jeremy Renner!"

This was a completely new experience. After posing for as many selfies as I could, I urged the kids to get to class before the second bell rang, but back at home that day I realized that it was one of the coolest things I'd ever experienced in my life.

My life changed that day—from not much liking my celebrity status I realized that I could use it for a real purpose, for good; finally, there was a value to it. I could have a real impact, and this aligned with my deepest love anyway, which is children. I'm the oldest of seven kids and it's part of my birthright to care about young people; I'd grown up that way, and it is a fundamental element of who I am.

Fast-forward to the summer of 2024 as we made our final preparations for Camp Rennervation. We'd had many partners contribute financially to make the place a great success. It's never easy asking people for money to support things like this, but it never mattered to me because I care way more about *action*—actually doing something screams love and it screams that someone cares. So here we were, all the people I love the most, ready to welcome the kids to camp. I was riding around the grounds on a golf cart, a huge Old Glory flying off the back, in cowboy boots, shorts, and a huge Stetson. Over by the dorms I saw Rory doing one last check; down by the lake, some volunteers were telling Dave that the kids were about to arrive. Kym and my mom and Nicky and Kayla were in the mess hall making sure the lunch was going to be ready for the kids when they deboarded the buses.

And then they arrived—110 kids, excited, probably a bit nervous, wide-eyed at the beautiful camp on the shores of Lake Tahoe. Waiting for each of these children (they ranged in age from eight to thirteen) were small roller suitcases with their names on them (so often in the foster care system kids show up at a new home with just a Hefty bag filled with their stuff). And we made each child a little fake passport—they had each moved around so much, we figured it would give them some agency to think of themselves as world travelers. There were books and games, and we'd expose them to nature and camaraderie and a drum circle and a huge barge of fireworks on the lake on July Fourth.

We just wanted to give them a homestead at least for a short time; a touchstone and community; something beautiful and memorable where the love I'd felt since childhood, the love that had only deepened since the incident, could be made flesh and shared with children most in need. These kids need to be heard, to be witnessed, to be understood; those were our goals.

This was action; *this* was love; *this* was the true legacy of the Pisten-Bully snowcat.

To me it's never really the big stuff—it's the small things. I take my survival, and my opportunities, as the greatest of blessings. It's my honor to have an impact on a kid's life, to be a voice for a kid, to inspire a kid. And it's my duty to have that positive impact. When it came to Camp Rennervation, I—along with all my friends and family—felt the power of that privilege every day we were there. So much so that what began as an annual thing is now expanding to be quarterly—we want the bonds between those kids that began on the shores of Lake Tahoe to be strengthened by regular chances to reconnect. (For some of the children, it was a rare chance to be with their siblings, who are sometimes placed in separate foster homes.)

I think everyone involved in that week had gone through a profound change in their lives already after the incident, and the camp only underlined what had changed. As Dave said to me, "This is our chance right now in life. I've totally reevaluated my priorities, my core values and passions. And to be able to witness up close and be a part of bringing joy and love to one hundred and ten foster kids was incredibly profound and rewarding and beautiful."

And there's a ripple effect beyond my inner circle, too—I see the results everywhere I look. As just one example, recently an actor friend called me after her father passed and asked me to talk to her about what I'd been through on the ice so that she could gain some peace imagining the journey her father was now on, given that I'd been on a similar journey, if only temporarily.

Then there was the couple in Milwaukee who contacted my sister about the RennerVation Foundation. They had long been foster parents, but tragically they had also lost their biological son around the same time I'd had my accident. In their grief they had followed my recovery closely and had gained some solace from it. In recent months the mother had gone through her own near-death experience in the hospital and had been amazed to discover that one of her nurses (a traveling nurse) had also worked with me at Renown. Everything was lining up, so much so that she and her husband committed to a huge donation to the RennerVation Foundation, a donation they plan to repeat every year going forward—this for a charity two thousand miles to their west.

No matter how prepared you are, if you check all the boxes in a crisis, you still need help. Love has to exist for people to be saved; that's what I was learning each time something like the Milwaukee donation happened.

As for me, I'm just happy to be a part of something that's much bigger than me. I don't have answers, I just know I'm part of something bigger, something collective, in perpetuity. We are so often privy to the worst versions of the world, but beyond the daily struggles—be it poverty, famine, war—there is still that intangible unity and divinity in all of us, all the time, which is magnificent and impermeable.

Even while you're reading this book, that ripple effect of love and care is happening. What an honor it is to be part of it, what a gift to be able to be thoughtful and loving to each other.

*   *   *

Someone asked me recently if surviving had made me a better or different actor, given that I'd been through so much, and I surprised myself with the answer. I used to use acting as a place to purge or express feelings, but now I'm wide open, so it may be that I'm neither better nor worse, but I'm certainly a very different actor now. Yes, I have more physical limitations on my body as an instrument, but my emotional world is fully taken up by my real life, so I noticed that when I first went back to work on *Mayor of Kingstown*, being in a fictional world felt a little frivolous, a little less powerful, at least at first. My new life is way more deeply rooted in the art of emotion—I now feel everything physically, mentally, emotionally, spiritually, and though sharing that is vulnerable and intimate, it's also honest, so even though there's heaviness to it, it's actually really light and freeing.

I used to give a shit about too many things and now I just don't. I have to get better first and everything else is going to fall into place. I won't burn out so fast now.

I sometimes joke that now I'm going to live forever, but even when my body one day gives out, I know my energy will go on.

*   *   *

As I said at the beginning, I did not want to write this book, but I'm happy I got out of my own way to share this experience with you.

If my healing has healed my family, perhaps there is a shot that it might be healing or inspiring for you, too. Either way, I am here because of you, so thank you.

The only thing I can control in my life is my perspective. What I've come to understand is that life is simply my next step, my next breath. Perhaps some readers might think that's too simple a philosophy, but I think life *is* that simple after all.

I am finally in the right place in my life; what happened that day, and the aftermath, served to redirect me into my life's purpose. But the incident didn't change me as much as it changed my role in my neighborhood, my city, the world. I've played a lot of roles, be they on-screen or off-, but now I feel like all those earlier roles prepared me for the role I was always meant to play: a father, a lover of people, a contributor to the well-being of my community.

So thank God for the glory moment. I now get to live a love-filled life, truly connected with people, trading handshakes for hugs. I've never been happier, never been more connected.

Thank God I died; and thank God I get to really live.

*   *   *

It is my blessing to be better every day. It took collective prayer and love to push me to my next breath, so it remains my duty to be better for all those who love me and all those who have helped me survive and recover.

I am better than I have even been, happier and more fulfilled and more deeply connected to those around me than I have ever known. I understand the privilege and the honor that brings, so I'm going to spend the rest of my years giving back the best I can.

I remain keenly aware that I'll never have a bad day for the rest of my life.

And to learn all that, all I had to do was die.

ACKNOWLEDGMENTS

An acknowledgment of the lifesaving efforts: Alex Fries, my brave nephew; Barb Fletcher and Rich Kovach, my neighbors; all the first responders; to my sister Kym and my entire family, who were there for me day and night by my side; to the long list of friends who tolerated me, supported me, and grew with me; to my community in Reno and Tahoe, who rallied for hope; and to all those whose prayers and goodwill were bestowed upon to me . . . I thank you. You all saved my life.

Very special thanks to Disney and Disney+, Marvel, Paramount, Creative Artists Agency, Megan Lynch and Flatiron Books, Lavazza, Truckee Meadows Fire and Rescue, North Lake Tahoe Fire Protection District, Washoe County Sheriff Darin Balaam, Reno Mayor Hillary Schieve, Renown hospital, the doctors and nurses of the Sierra ICU, Dr. Jo Wedell, Dr. Peter Althausen, supervisor nurse Angie, social worker Abbie Smith, Whitney Hansen, REMSA Care Flight team, Eldorado Reno Hotel and Casino and the Carano family, Rick Murdoch, the Cedars-Sinai doctors and entire ICU team, Dr. Dan Margulies, Dr. John Garlich, Dr. Iman

Rabizadeh, Dr. Andrew Wang, Dr. Jay Lee, Dr. Benjamin Walline, Maria De Sio, Dr. Gary Tearston, Dr. Charles Sophy, Dr. Christopher Vincent, Dr. Jamie Milnes, Dr. Erica Lehman, Ralph Lim, and Brian Enyart Sr.

Further thanks to Technogym.com; Powerplate.com; Boost Treadmills, boosttreadmills.com; Achilles, anklerepair.com; Specialized Bikes, specialized.com; Nice Recovery, nicerecovery.com; Normatec, hyperice. com; Icetubs.com; Clearlight.com; B-Strong, bstrong.training; Oura, ouraring.com; Muhdo.com; and Affordable Hyperbaric Solutions.

ABOUT THE AUTHOR

JEREMY LEE RENNER is a two-time Academy Award–nominated actor who has earned critical acclaim for his work in both independent cinema and major blockbusters, solidifying his reputation as one of Hollywood's most dynamic actors. Renner first gained widespread attention with his portrayal of Jeffrey Dahmer in *Dahmer*; he later delivered a breakout performance in *The Hurt Locker* as an adrenaline-driven bomb disposal expert, earning his first Academy Award nomination, for Best Actor. His role in *The Town*, as a fiercely loyal yet dangerous bank robber, garnered him a second Oscar nomination, for Best Supporting Actor.

In recent years Renner has starred in two *Mission: Impossible* movies and *The Bourne Legacy* and has garnered both critical acclaim and wide popularity for his portrayal of Clint Barton, aka Hawkeye, in the Marvel Cinematic Universe and the Disney+ series *Hawkeye*. Currently, Renner stars in *Mayor of Kingstown* as Mike McLusky, navigating the gritty and morally complex world of prison systems and small-town politics.

Outside of acting, Renner is a talented musician, philanthropist, and entrepreneur. His RennerVation Foundation repurposes disused vehicles for the needs of the wider community across the United States and the world and runs regular recreational camps for children in foster care in Nevada. This is his first book.